The Annals of Blantyre

By Rev Stewart Wright - 1885

Transcribed by Paul D Veverka

A Blantyre Project Publication

The Annals of Blantyre

First Published 1885

Copyright © 2017 by The Blantyre Project

All rights Reserved by transcription author, Paul D Veverka

Cover Photo: "Blantyre Manse 1950s, former home of Stewart Wright"

ISBN 10: 1539965775
ISBN-13: 978-1539965770

DEDICATION

This book is dedicated not just to Rev. Stewart Wright (dec) who wrote this book, but also to all the clergy of Blantyre both past and present, for their efforts, their dedication, faith in God and in humanity.

Figure 1 Livingstone's Birthplace

The Annals of Blantyre

CONTENTS

	Contents	Page 5
	Foreword	Page 9
	About the Author	Page 11
1	Ecclesiastical (i) to (vii)	Page 13
2	Civil (i) to (v)	Page 45
3	Eminent Men	Page 67
4	Natural History	Page 81
5	Miscellaneous	Page 91
	Appendix	Page 123
	About the Transcriber	Page 127

The Annals of Blantyre

By Rev Stewart Wright

LIST OF ILLUSTRATIONS

House where Livingstone was born	Page 3
Clyde between Bothwell Castle & Blantyre Priory	Page 16
Old Parish Church	Page 33
New Parish Church	Page 44
Erskine House	Page 79
Bridge at Milheugh	Page 106

The Annals of Blantyre

By Rev Stewart Wright

FOREWORD

The 'Annals of Blantyre' was first published in 1885 but fell out of publication in the early 20th Century. Being specifically about the history of Blantyre, South Lanarkshire, Scotland, the book had a specific interest, primarily to the people of Blantyre and has been enjoyed by several generations. However, remaining copies of the original book are few and far between, but can still be found from time to time in auction markets, online on auction websites and the odd copy in local libraries.

Paul Veverka of the community history archive, 'Blantyre Project' has set out to republish this old book by transcribing it exactly as it was written in 1885, together with the original illustrations and making the book available to readers again in an affordable manner. All financial proceeds from the purchase of this book are going to local Blantyre charities and good causes.

The cover photo of the former High Blantyre Manse was the home of Rev. Stewart Wright, the original author of this book and it is in those rooms that he likely wrote this book.

The Annals of Blantyre

ABOUT THE AUTHOR

Rev. Stewart Wright was a former minister of High Blantyre Old Parish Church for 16 years from 1871 until 1887. He was the second minister to preach from the this Old Parish Church, which still exists today at Main Street. Stewart Wright was admitted to this charge on 3rd August 1871.

Born in Inverary, Argyll on 15th October 1829, Stewart was the fifth son of James Wright who at one point was provost of the Argyleshire town. Mr. Wright received his education at Inverary, Irvine Academy and the Universities of Glasgow and Edinburgh.

He was licensed by Glasgow Presbytery and was for a time assistant at St. Mathews, Glasgow. On 23rd May 1855 he was ordained and inducted to the charge of St. George's in the Fields. Thereafter, abroad he was chaplain at Madras from 1858 - 1865 and at Bangalore from 1865 - 1871.

On 3rd January 1856 Mr. Wright married Alice, the daughter of the Rev. Colin Smith D.D, the minister of Inverary. They had twelve of a family. 4 boys and 8 girls but sadly, at least 4 of the family died in infancy or early childhood something, which must have been heartbreaking beyond words.

He is not on the 1871 census, as he was still in India but came to Blantyre Parish a few months after. In the 1875 Valuation Book, he is noted as being the owner of the Manse at High Blantyre and also the Glebe (Manse) Land. The assessor valued the manse as being worth a rent of £25/year and the land at £22/year, something that reflects how substantial this house and land was by comparison to the properties around it.

There can be very little doubt that the Rev. Stewart Wright was highly thought of in this parish and we must bear in mind that his work here must have been very difficult especially after that awful Monday morning of the 22nd October, 1877 when "*in a moment, in the twinkling of an eye*" over two hundred men and boys were killed in the Blantyre Pit Explosion. It fell to Mr. Wright to minister to the desperate needs of the people - some 106 widows, 300 fatherless children and about 50 other bereaved relatives. He described himself as "a stricken shepherd amongst a stricken flock". We note in passing at this point that on 29th June 1880 a new "Chapel of Ease" was opened in Blantyre. Later to become known as Stonefield Parish this "*Chapel of Ease*" remained under Blantyre Parish Church until 1890 when it was raised to a "*Quoad Sacra*" Parish with its own Kirk Session. Rev Stewart Wright attended the opening.

In the 1881 census, Stewart was 51 years old; living at the Kirkton manse, High Blantyre with wife, Alice aged 46. With them were 6 children. Mary HS Wright 21, Jeanie GS Wright 17, William NS Wright 12, Elizabeth S Wright 12, Flora MS Wright 10, Dora S Wright 8. The 4 eldest children were all born in India. Flora was born in Bridge of Allan and only little Dora was a Blantyre girl. In 1881, the family had lodgers at the manse, which was sizeable. Mr. Michael Brogan aged 41 was an unemployed engine man formerly working at Colin Dunlop's Colliery. Mr Ralph Fairbarin aged 33 also a labourer at the aforementioned colliery, Helen Simpson a 21-year old domestic servant and Jane M Birrell, a 19-year old nanny for children William, Elizabeth and Dora.

Rev Wright was of course the original author of this book, "The Annals of Blantyre". He was a remarkable, well travelled man who gave us such a unique look at Blantyre's 19th Century past. The book is written in the same language and spelling that Stewart Wright adtoped, often using Scots terms less frequently used today. The transcription following aligns with that deliberate style. A year later in 1886, his 4th child, a daughter Elizabeth Stewart Wright died aged 17 and was buried in High Blantyre Cemetery. Losing a fifth child of the twelve he had may have pushed Stewart's heartache to breaking point, and other men may have questioned the work of god upon such instances. Rev Wright remained steadfast in his faith.

His health failing, Stewart died soon after on the 29th November 1887. His will was read on 21st March the following year, his estate worth £619 9s 5d left entirely to his surviving widow, Alice. His daughter Dora Stewart Wright died in 1932 and was buried in High Blantyre Cemetery aged 59. His son William Stewart Wright died on 20th April 1944 aged 56. Passing away so soon after this book was written, it is unfortunate that Stewart Wright never knew the impact and popularity it would have amongst not just Blantyre readers, but those much further afield too.

CHAPTER 1

Ecclesiastical

I.

In the first printed statistical account of Blantyre, which was written about a hundred years ago by one of our predecessors, the Rev. Henry Stevenson, minister of Blantyre, we find that he ascribes the origin of the name to the sheltered situation of the locality; Blantyre being said to signify in the Gaelic language, a *warm retreat.* We are not prepared to accept this derivation, for to our own mind and judging from our experience, the parish, as a whole, can scarcely be characterised as a warm retreat. It has certainly got its sheltered nooks by the banks of the Clyde and Calder, where pleasant mansions nestle amongst wooded groves; but we fear that the general verdict on the climate of our parish now-a-days will be somewhat akin to that of the poet's shivering traveller —

> "Cold blows the wind across the moor,
> The dreary moor that I have passed."

And so accepting not the derivation given by Mr. Stevenson, we would venture on another one which appears to us much more appropriate. It is this — Blantyre is derived from the two Gaelic words that signify *"the field of the holy men,"* for the parish was, to a very large extent, the *property of the Church.* The first mention of it is in some ancient records, where it is spoken of as belonging to the Abbacy of Jedburgh; the abbot and the monks of which had formed a sort of colony, and here they built their Priory as a "cell," or retreat for themselves, when compelled to fly from the Borderland during the many bloody wars that raged for centuries between the English and the Scotch. Hence the natural origin of the name Blantyre, the field of the holy men.

And now for its early ecclesiastical history — very meagre indeed, but not uninteresting. We cannot tell the exact year when the Priory was built, but we know that it must have been in existence considerably before 1289, for there is mention made in one of the old Statute Books of a Prior of Blantyre being present at a Parliament which was held at Briggeham sometime during that year; and "*Frere William Priour de Blantyre*" is likewise alluded to as "a subscriber to Bagimond's Roll," where the Priory is taxed upon a valuation of £66 13s. 4d.

This same Prior swore fealty to Edward I of England at Berwick, 28th August, 1296.

Our readers will not object to being enlightened upon what this "*Bagimond's Roll*" was. In order to carry out the Crusade against the Saracens, upon which he was determined, Pope Innocent IV was obliged to put forth great exertions. Accordingly, in the year 1254, he granted to Henry III of England a twentieth part of the Ecclesiastical Revenues of Scotland for three years, provided he would join the crusade. In 1268, Pope Clement IV renewed this grant, and increased it to a tenth, but when Henry attempted to levy the tax the Scottish clergy resisted and appealed to Rome. But the appeal was of no avail. Henry was promised the money, and he required it, for already his gallant son was at the head of an English army on their way to the Holy Land.

Accordingly, the Pope sent a special messenger to Scotland to collect the tithes or tenth of all the Ecclesiastical benefices. This emissary was one Baiamund de Vicci, better known amongst us as *Bagimund*. Again the Clergy protested and sent back the collector to Rome. But the Pope was inexorable; he insisted upon the hated tax. Of course, the levying of it was troublesome and difficult, so much so that "Bull" after "Bull" had to be thundered from Rome to bring the Scotch clergy and people to a proper obedience. This undoubtedly was one of the chief stimulants to the arrogant assumptions of the English King over the kingdom of Scotland, which soon afterwards aroused the injured nation to fight for their liberties and "lay the proud usurper low." Such is the story about "Bagimond's Roll."

There is one other mention in those old worm — eaten records of a Prior of Blantyre, which shows that these ecclesiastics were wont to take a prominent part in the Councils of the nation, for "Prior Walter of Blantyre was one of the Scottish Commissioners appointed to negotiate the ransom of King David Bruce, taken prisoner in the battle of Durham, in the year 1346."

For a considerable time before the Reformation, the appointment of the Priors of Blantyre appears to have belonged to the Archbishops of

By Rev Stewart Wright

Glasgow, and during the vacancy of that See the right was exercised by the Crown. Thus we find that on the 24th September, 1547, John Roull, Prior of Pittenweem, obtained a presentation to the Priory of Blantyre, vacant by the death of Mr John Moncrief; and on the 6th of October, 1549, John, son of David Hamilton of Bothwellhaugh, was presented to the Priory on the resignation of Mr John Roull; the presentation being with the Queen, owing to the vacancy of the See of Glasgow.

Such is the amount of information of any interest that can now be gleaned as to the religious establishment in Blantyre before the Reformation. That time came and its work. John Knox thundered over the length and breadth of the land, "*Pull down the nests and the rooks will fly away,*" and right loyally his mandate was obeyed. Like many other more stately edifices, our old Priory fell before the blows of the Reformers. James VI, of pious memory, suppressed the order, and bestowed the benefice and lands upon his well-beloved cousin and companion in early days, Walter Stuart, who was Treasurer of Scotland in the year 1595, and afterwards created a Peer by the title of Lord Blantyre, 10th July, 1606.

As some of our readers may not know the exact locality where stood the Blantyre Priory, the approach to its scattered ruins having been closed for years to the public, let us inform them that it was built on a high rock which rises perpendicularly from the Clyde, and directly opposite to the majestic ruins of Bothwell Castle.

The following is a graphic description of the surrounding scenery, which we lately came across, but by whom written we cannot tell.

"The Clyde here is a majestic river, of considerable depth, and of a darkish colour, gliding smoothly and silently along between the lofty wooded banks, and beautiful and richly adorned undulating fields of Bothwell and Blantyre. Immediately below Bothwell Bridge the banks present a thin sprinkling of wood with occasional orchards. About a mile and a half farther down in a snug retreat almost concealed by the rising grounds on either side, the lofty walls of Blantyre Works appear; where a busy population, and the rushing noise of machinery contrast strangely with the silence and repose of the surrounding scenery, and seem as if intended to bring into competition the works of Nature and of art. The lofty woods of Bothwell on the east and of Blantyre on the west, with the magnificent red walls and circular towers of the old Castle of Bothwell, and the shattered remains of Blantyre Priory on the opposite side on the summit of a lofty rock add greatly to the beauty of the scenery. A little further on, the banks begin to decline before they reach

Daldowie, and the river leaves the parish amid fertile fields and wide expanding haughs. The whole on a summer day when the sun is shining is inexpressibly beautiful."

Figure 2 The Clyde between Bothwell Castle & Blantyre Priory

II.

In the old days of the "Papacy" when the abbots and canons of Jedburgh were wont to find a sure refuge and warm retreat in their beautiful Priory, the village of Blantyre was situated not far distant from them in a lovely undulating field which forms a long narrow peninsula between the rivers Clyde and Calder. We can scarcely conceive of a brighter and more pleasant spot. It is left to our imagination what it must have been in those olden times when there was no "roar of machinery" to drown the murmurings of the flowing river, and no shriek of a passing engine to break the deep silence of Bothwell's bonny braes. And what with be stags that bounded through the woods and the salmon and trout that swarmed in their rivers, the jolly priests and peaceful villagers of that old Blantyre must have felt that verily their lines had fallen in pleasant places, and that theirs was a goodly heritage.

But, alas! for us that heritage is gone, and salmon and stags are to be found no more! Of this old village of which we speak not one stone now remains; only a few green hillocks tell of the huts where the humble people lived, and some scattered fragments of tombstones betoken their last resting places when their simple lives had ended.

Professor Wilson, our famous Christopher North, who spent some portion of his joyous youth in this locality, takes a poet's license when in one of his exquisite "Tales" he speaks of the "ladies of Calder Cottage" being buried in this old burying ground, which he designates as "the sweet churchyard of Blantyre that was only a few hundred yards distant from their flowery and shaded home." We may be certain that the daisies which grow in that old "God's acre" have not been disturbed to receive any mouldering remains of humanity for three hundred years and more. It is perfectly legitimate for us to conjecture that when the Priory fell before the sweeping power of the Reformation, and its priestly inmates were driven hence, their former dependents and retainers wisely conformed to the new order of things and left their homes, pleasant though they were, on the banks of the Clyde, to migrate into the interior of the parish and help to build that picturesque village of "Kirkton," which still surrounds the Parish Church of Blantyre.

That this supposition is highly probable we may aver from the almost universal ecclesiastical custom of the sheep following their shepherd, for it is a pleasant fact to state that the last Roman Catholic Prior of Blantyre embraced the principles of the Reformation and became the first Protestant minister of the parish. The name of this worthy man was William Chirnsyde.

He had been "Provost" of the Collegiate Church of Bothwell, but this Provostry he exchanged for the Priory of Blantyre on the 3rd of September, 1552, when it became vacant by the resignation of John, son of David Hamilton of Bothwellhaugh, who, four years preceding this, had received the presentation to the Priory from the unfortunate Mary "Queen of Scots."

In another chapter we will trace the history of our Church and Parish subsequent to the Reformation, and, thanks to an eminent antiquarian, we can do this very perfectly, having received the name and much of the history of every minister of Blantyre since that period. At present we shall only allude to the original Parish Church and the old "Communion Cups." As many of our readers are aware, the site of this church was in the middle of the burying ground at Kirkton, now closed, but which for centuries has received the dead of Blantyre. Tradition affirms that the church was both a beautiful and substantial structure, its style of architecture being somewhat akin to that of the neighbouring Parish Church of Bothwell. That it was a "holy and beautiful house" we can well believe, for it was built long prior to that period when, under Puritanical influences, unseemly barns were substituted for ecclesiastical edifices, and its solidity has ample testimony in the simple fact that it stood as a "House of God" until towards the close of the last century; and we venture to affirm that if it had been properly cared for it might have been standing to this day. Our predecessor, Mr Stevenson, thus writes of it in the year 1785: — "There is no record of the time when the church was built. It bears evident marks of great antiquity and is in a most deplorable condition." Seven years afterwards the Presbytery of Hamilton condemned the building as unsafe and unfit for worship owing to decay and rottenness, and so it was pulled down and another one, very unlike in many respects, was erected upon its site.

Not many are aware of the most interesting relics of those bygone times, which we still have in our possession, in our "Communion Cups." A few years ago we received a communication from a gentleman in Edinburgh who devotes himself to antiquarian researches, in which he requested that we would kindly send to him the "trade mark" which was cut on the silver cups which were still in use at Blantyre at the Holy

Communion, as he had heard they were of great age. We gladly responded to his request, and were soon gratified with the following information: — "The Blantyre cups were made in Edinburgh some time between the years 1550 and 1570, as they bear the initials of the Deacon of the Gold and Silver-smiths Guild during that period. With one exception, they are the oldest cups in Scotland, and that one exception is the cups in the parish of Fyvie in Aberdeenshire."

Are they not interesting memorials those silver cups, which happily are still ours? What a "cloud of witnesses" seem to rise up around them! Think of the long period of their existence, over three hundred years! How many the generations, so to speak, that they have seen come and go — a long ceaseless train passing and ever passing onwards to the grave. How many the trembling hands that have lifted those cups to trembling lips? How often have been re-echoed over them by pastor after pastor the words of the Good Shepherd who laid down His life for the sheep — "This cup is the new testament in my blood: this do ye as oft as ye drink it in remembrance of me." Be it ours to use these memorials "worthily," and as our fathers have handed them down to us, may we hand them down to our children and children's children with the affectionate admonition — Prize these, and hear the grand old story which they tell of the love of Jesus Christ, so that this love may constrain you to live not unto yourselves but unto Him who died for you and rose again.

III.

The year 1567 is an ever memorable year in the history of the Scottish church and nation; for, towards the close of it, on the 15th of December, the Parliament met, and after having accepted the resignation of Queen Mary, who was then a prisoner in Loch Leven Castle, and given its sanction to the coronation of James and the regency of Moray, it passed a series of acts directly affecting the national religion.

The Parliament of August, 1560, had never received the royal sanction, and, therefore, it was deemed prudent to re-enact its enactments. "The jurisdiction of the Pope was abolished; all laws in favour of the Roman Catholic religion were repealed; the Protestant Confession of Faith was ratified and engrossed in the records; and the saying and hearing of Mass was declared to be a crime punishable with confiscation of goods for the first offence, banishment for the second, death for the third."

Legislation proceeded still farther, and declared the Church now established to be the only true Church of Christ, and that every future Sovereign of the Kingdom must swear, at his coronation, before the Eternal God to maintain this reformed National Church. Thus was Protestantism established in the land. It was in this year of 1567, as we have already said, that the Rev. William Chirnsyde, the last Romish prior of Blantyre, casting in his lot with the reformers, became the first minister of the parish, and such he continued to be till the year 1572, when he was translated to the parish of Luss, in Dumbartonshire.

His successor appointed, two years afterwards, in 1574, was a Mr John Davidson. This minister appears to have enjoyed a plurality of livings: for, during several years, he held the benefices of Hamilton, Dalserf, Cambuslang, and Blantyre. But certainly his remuneration for this multiplicity of work was not very great. His stipend amounted to £133 6s 8d, of which £27 15s 6d was out of the "third" of the Priory of Blantyre. Of course, as Mr Davidson was not ubiquitous, and able to officiate at one and the same time in his various charges, he required to have assistants, so we find that Mr John Hamilton was then "reader" at Blantyre, with a stipend of £16 and the Kirkland. The fact is, that for very many years subsequent to the Reformation there was a great scarcity of ministers. Thirty-six years after it there were upwards of 400 churches throughout Scotland unsupplied with Protestant preachers. From the register of ministers and their stipends in 1567, it would appear that there were then about 1080 churches under the charge of 257 ministers, 151 exhorters, and 455 readers. Certainly many of the Romish clergy, like Mr Chirnsyde, became Protestant ministers, but it is certain that many more would have joined the ranks of the reformers were it not for their great dislike to become "preachers."

Evidently preaching was not in their line, as perhaps it entailed too much work. Then the laity in those days could send up few recruits to the holy office of the ministry: for learning was confined to a very small circle of the community, and, to the shame of those mighty ones who had seized upon the rich revenues of the Church, be it recorded, that the stipends given to the first Protestants ministers were so small and so badly paid when due that few were induced to enter into "Holy orders," and many were compelled, from starvation, to abandon their vocation. Melville, in his diary, speaks of some ballads which had been made against those who had thus deserted their calling —

>"Who so do put hand to the pleuche,
>And therefra backward goes;
>The Scripture makes it plain aneuch,
>My Kingdom is not for those," etc.

Very true, Mr Rhymer, but what can a man or a minister do if the labourer receives not his hire? He must even leave the "pleuche" and betake himself to some other vocation that will prove itself more generous and just. Thus, it is not to be wondered at that in those days it was a very general thing that three or four parishes should have been under the care of one minister. Indeed, it is alleged that the "good Regent" Moray favoured this paucity of *ministers* and multiplicity of *readers:* for, as the former were paid 200 merks, and the latter but 20 merks, there was thus a great saving of the revenues of the State, although a further spoliation of the revenues of the Church!

In the year 1591, Mr Davidson, this pluralist, died, and was succeded in Blantyre by Mr John Brown, formerly at Neilston. This minister appears to have held the living only for two years. What became of him is not recorded. His successor was a young "graduate" of Glasgow – Mr William Boyd, A.M. No doubt this superior scholar was likewise a popular preacher, if we may judge of those olden times by our own: for he was not allowed to remain long in Blantyre, having received and accepted a call in the following year to the parish of Glenluce, in the Presbytery of Stranraer.

The vacancy at Blantyre was filled up by the appointment of Mr John Sangstare, who was translated from the neighbouring parish of Glasford. He continued minister for fifteen years, when he died November, 1609, leaving "Helen Hamilton, relict, and three daughters – Elspeth, Marion, and Christian," also an inventory of his "guids" at the time of his decease. This document has been preserved, why or wherefore we cannot tell, except for the laudable purpose of gratifying the curiosity of succeeding generations. We will therefore make no apologies for giving our readers some of the "items" of the *"Minister's will"* in 1609. He bequeathed – "Ane tydie cow, price £14 Scots; ane quey of three yeir auld, price £16 13s 4d; item, ane stack of aitts in the barn yard extending to 28 threaves, estimate to 8 bolls, price of the boll with the fodder, £5, Inde (total), £40; certain pease, estimate to 3 bolls, price of the boll, £3 6s 8d, Inde, £10; item, ane feather bed in his Chalmer in Hamilton, price £6 13s 4d; item, in Blantyre, ane standard bed of aik, price £6 6s 8d; item, ane meal almerie, price £10; item, ane meikle kist, worth £5 6s 8d; item, ane lettrom (reading desk), price £2; item, twa chyres (chairs), price of them baith, £4 13s 4d; item, ane new girdle, price £3 6s 8d; item, ane masking fat, in the custody of Robert Hamilton in Priestfield, worth 40s; item, twa barrells, price 26s 8d ; item, ane cloak and gown, and the rest of the abuljements of his body, estimate to be worth £40; item, his haill buiks, meikle and little, estimate to be worth other £40 – summa, £190 6s 8d."

Such are some of the items of the "Minister's will"; but like all other wills, ancient and modern, it has got a sting in the tail of it: for the "reading" of it must have fallen heavily upon the heart of a gentleman therein mentioned. It ends thus :— "He never made promise to William Naismyth, his son-in-law, of any particular tocher or soums of money, but as he micht he wald, and nae farder he wald do to him." Poor man! it is to be hoped that he did not indulge in great expectations, for evidently he was cut off with a shilling – and a Scotch shilling in those days was worth but a *penny*.

IV.

On the death of Mr Sangstare, whom we shall kindly remember as the bequeather of "The Will," in the year 1609, Mr John Heriot, M.A., of Glasgow University, was appointed his successor. This is a name familiar to most of our parishioners, at all events to the natives of the parish; for who of them have not oftentimes, in boyhood and in age, strayed into the old "kirk yard" and read on a large flat tombstone the following inscription and poetry: –

"Here lies the corpse of Mr John Heriot, who was a Minister of God's Word in the Parish of Blantyre for the space of 55 years: his age 90, who died the 7th day of December, 1665."

> *"Here lies a pastor ten years and four score,*
> *Who taught his flock 55 years and more*
> *During which time, to his immortal praise,*
> *So blamelessly behaved himself always*
> *In holy order, doctrine Sweet and sound,*
> *As did become his reverend gospel gown.*
> *His soul in heaven, his body in the clay,*
> *Wait a reunion at the latter day."*

We must not here omit to mention that this tombstone which marks the resting-place of the worthy Mr Heriot was renewed a few years ago by the late Mr Scott of Blantyre Farm.

Our readers will be not a little surprised when we inform them that from the year 1609, when Mr. Heriot was ordained, to the year 1689, when the Revolution took place on the landing of William and Mary, the ministers of Blantyre, with one exception, were willingly or unwillingly Prelatists: that is to say, they obeyed the laws of the Parliaments of the Stuarts, acknowledged the rule of the Bishops, and accepted the Episcopal form of Government, if not likewise the Episcopal form of worship.

The tradition of the parish is, as we have often heard from old residents, that Mr. Heriot was the last of the "Episcopalian" ministers; but Ecclesiastical Records still in existence show that three, if not four, of his successors were "Curates," the last of whom was deprived of the living when Episcopacy in Scotland fell with the dynasty of the Stuarts, and

Presbyterianism became triumphant. This accounts for the remarkable circumstance that during all those dismal years, when the fires of persecution burned so terribly in the neighbouring parishes, they approached not to Blantyre.

The "Cloud of Witnesses" makes mention of men belonging to Hamilton, Bothwell, East Kilbride, Glasford, Strathaven, etc., who fell in the battles between the Cavaliers and Covenanters, or who were taken prisoners after the fatal day of Bothwell Brig, and banished to America or the West Indies; but we have failed to find the name of a single parishioner of Blantyre. And only one appears in the "Fugitive Roll" of 1684, namely, "Andrew Reid, servitor to Robert Smith at Blantyre Kirk," who is denounced as a rebel and fugitive. True, indeed, the inhabitants of the parish must have been then very few, but it cannot be doubted that the "conforming" ministers helped to keep them obedient and quiet: so the cyclone raged around them, but peace was within their borders. We here state facts; we make no comment, whatever, of approval or disapproval, of the action of our predecessors. But to return to the *role* of ministers.

Mr. Heriot lived to a great age, but long before his death, which was so much lamented by his people, as the gravestone still testifies, he was unfit for duty, and so had colleagues and assistants. The first of these was Mr. Hew Mitchell, who was appointed in the year 1636, and held office until 1653, when he either died or was transferred to another parish. He was succeeded by Mr. James Hamilton, M.A., of Glasgow University. This young minister, hailing as he did from the stronghold of the Covenanters, the districts of Lesmahagow and Strathaven, held strong Presbyterian principles, and acted upon them, so he speedily came into contact with the stern powers that then ruled. Refusing to "conform," he was deprived of his living by an Act of Parliament, 11th June, 1662, which was ratified by the Privy Council on the 10th of October of the same year. Continuing pertinacious, he was never reinstated, although he lived for many years afterwards. His future career in life was rather chequered. Seven years after his deprivation, in 1669, he was imprisoned for preaching in his own house to his family and others, and was detained till his health was impaired when he was, liberated on the application of his brother, Sir Robert Hamilton of Silvertonhill, on a bond of 1000 merks for compearance. He was "indulged" at Strathaven by the Privy Council on the 3rd September, 1672, but again in 1678 he was rebuked for intruding on his own parish and dismissed. He continued to live at Strathaven till 1684. In justice to the memory of Mr. Hamilton, we must briefly allude to the noble defence which he made of himself when arraigned before the Chancellor and a Committee of Council in Edinburgh, as recorded in Wodrow's history.

When driven from Blantyre, Mr Hamilton went to reside in Glasgow, where, in "his own house," he preached the Gospel. This was the offence charged against him by the Archbishop and Provost of Glasgow, who sent him under a strong guard to the capital city to stand his trial. When interrogated if the charge was true, and how many hearers he was wont to have, he answered, that these years bygone, when poor ministers of Christ were forced from their flocks, and with difficulty enough were able to subsist themselves and families, they had no money to hire palaces and castles to live in, and their lordships might easily guess that any house he was able to take could not contain great numbers of hearers; neither could he keep people from coming to his house, having no halberts to keep his doors nor guards to make use of. Some of the members of committee upbraided him for reflecting on the Archbishop of Glasgow, and attempted to impress him with a due sense of the lenity and favour of his lordship in permitting him to reside so long within his diocese. Mr Hamilton answered — It is very easy to speak of lenity and favour, but he was assured he had not so much lenity and favour in Glasgow as Paul enjoyed under a violent persecuting heathen ruler at Rome, where he remained two whole years preaching the Gospel in his own hired house, and no man was forbid to come to him; whereas the honest people of Glasgow and himself had been threatened with great violence if they did forbear. Finding that they were not likely to gain any ground on him by their queries, they desired to know if he was willing for the time to come to give bond to preach no more this way. His reply was that he had his commission from Christ to preach the Gospel, and he would not take any restrictions upon himself, whatever force others might bring him under. The Chancellor was pleased to ask him where his commission was. He replied— "Matthew xxviii. 19: Go, teach and baptize." The Chancellor sneeringly said — "That is the Apostles' commission; and do you set up for an apostle?" "No, my lord," was the dignified reply of the accused, "not an apostle, nor any extraordinary person either; but that is the commission of ordinary ministers of the Gospel as well as extraordinary ambassadors, such as were the Apostles." Noble man! persecuted for righteousness' sake; all worthy art thou to stand in the foremost rank side by side with the goodly fellowship of the prophets and the glorious company of the apostles and the noble army of martyrs. Mr. Hamilton was remanded to prison, where he lay for a long time, until, as we have already said, his brother made interest on his behalf, and effected his release, after his health had considerably failed. The three next ministers of Blantyre after Mr. Hamilton were "curates." On his being cast out for nonconformity, Mr. Richard Brown received the appointment, which he held only for a year, when he was translated to the parish of Biggar.

His successor was a James Berrie, who was translated from a parish in Aberdeenshire, which "far away" shire seems to have been in those days a hotbed for the rearing of curates. Mr Berrie was ordained to Blantyre on the 26th April, 1666, and continued its minister until his death, in April, 1678, at the age of 59. We are told, as an interesting piece of intelligence, that "he had a daughter Agnes, who was infeft in liferent of houses and lands in the Kirtoun of Blantyre, on 26th July, 1677."

The next incumbent of Blantyre was another north-country man. He was George Leslie, M.A., who took his degree at King's College, Aberdeen, in 1670. He passed trials before the Presbytery of Paisley, and got testimonials for license in 1677. He continued in Blantyre from 1679 to 1689, the year of the Revolution, when he shared the hard fate with more than 200 fellow curates of "being evicted from their manses and parishes and livings." No doubt these men with their wives and families suffered much; many of them must have been rendered homeless; some of them reduced to absolute beggary; and it is sad to read in the records of the kirk-sessions of that period of small sums of money being given to an "Episcopal minister" or a "poor curate's wife." Still, let us not forget that the now dominant Presbyterians had for many years been a persecuted people in their own country. They were made to suffer more than the mere loss of worldly goods; theirs were bonds and imprisonments, scourgings and tortures, diverse and cruel deaths. It is pleasant therefore to record that when the day of reckoning came, they did not rise up to avenge their wrongs in a wholesale murdering of their oppressors. Still, let us not conceal the fact that those times of which we write were very turbulent, and whatever party was in the ascendant, their actions were not generally characterised by tolerance and mercifulness.

V.

The wholesale evictions of the curates necessarily caused many vacancies, and to fill these up with suitable men must have proved for some time a great difficulty. Blantyre got a minister from the north of Ireland; his name was Robert Landesse, and his ordination took place on the 12th August, 1690. This appointment, however, was not effected without a small fight. The Presbytery of Antrim sent a letter to the Presbytery of Hamilton, 20th January, 1691, inviting the return of Mr Landesse to the parish of Ballymoney, alleging his relation to that parish to be yet standing. The Presbytery judging "the relation to be loosed, returned an answer to the said letter." Then the Synod of Belfast took up the matter, and wrote a peremptory letter to the Presbytery demanding the return of the runaway minister, "considering the paucity of ministers in their bounds, and the legal right which they have to him as a Co-Presbyter." Still the Presbytery declined, and appointed a committee to answer the said letter. And so Mr Landesse was permitted to remain at Blantyre, where he performed the duties of his office until the end of 1702, when he demitted the charge on account of his age. We must mention that before his appointment to Blantyre Mr Landesse had been imprisoned in Edinburgh for six weeks: his crime being non-conformity.

The successor to Mr Landesse was Mr Matthew Connell, who was licensed by the Presbytery of Glasgow in 1702, and ordained to Blantyre on the 12th April, 1704. Sixteen years afterwards, in 1720, he was translated to East Kilbride. This gentleman was known by the soubriquet of "Mass Connell." Why he was so we may perhaps safely ascribe to some "High Church" or Prelatical proclivities apparent in his mode of conducting the public worship. The same name is still oftentimes applied by the Irish peasantry to their priests. Mr Connell had some sons, who, like many other "sons of the manse," acted well their part in life. One of them entered into the holy office of the ministry and became his father's assistant and successor. He continued minister of East Kilbride for very many years. Another son was the Right Honourable Arthur Connell, Lord Provost of Glasgow in the years 1772-73. This gentleman and his sons were prominent West India merchants during the last century, and helped to lay the foundation of the great city of which we are so justly proud. We quote the following from "Curiosities of Glasgow Citizenship:" — "The famous old firm, latterly known as Stirling, Gordon & Co., was founded about the middle of last century by Provost Arthur Connell and James Somerville of Hamilton Farm, under the title of Somerville, Connell & Co.

In 1790 the name of the firm was changed to Stirling, Gordon & Co., and the chief partners at that time were the well-known John Gordon of Aitkenhead, his brother Alexander, and John Stirling of Kippendavie, whose father was an extensive Jamaica merchant, and left his son a large fortune. The firm was very prosperous, and consisted of gentlemen whose names in the latter part of last century were a household word, and who are yet known as the chief of the old Glasgow aristocracy." Furthermore, let it be recorded of this worthy "son of the manse," Provost Arthur Connell, that not only was he amongst the chief of the Glasgow merchant princes, but that he continued, until his death, one of the most respected "ruling elders;" and the records of the Town Council bear witness that, on the 7th of April, 1774, he was "unanimously elected the representative of the city to the General Assembly of the Church about to meet in Edinburgh." But to return to our parish.

Mr. Matthew Connell was succeeded in Blantyre by the Rev. Richard Henderson, M.A. of Glasgow University. He was ordained on the 1st of August, 1722, and continued minister of the parish for the long period of forty-eight years. He died on the 12th December, 1769, in the eightieth year of his age. His widow, Jane Cleland, lived after him until November, 1784. They left two sons — Archibald, who became a merchant in Glasgow; and Alexander, who went to Virginia. The following reference to the following is another interesting quotation from the "Curiosities:" — "Archibald Henderson was a well known Virginia merchant, and chairman of Commerce in 1787. His firm of Archibald Henderson & Co. was among the leading tobacco importers when the Chamber was founded. As a member of the Hodge-Podge Club, he has a stanza in Dr. Moore's famous song of the Club. It speaks of him as 'Begot, born, and bred in John Calvin's meek faith.' He was a son of the Rev. Archd. Henderson of Blantyre. What the father's views had been may be gathered from his having been one of the few ministers who gave a hand to Whitfield in the 'Cambuslang Wark.' What the son's were may be gathered from Dr. Moore's verses. Archibald Henderson has descendants from a son who settled in Virginia; but he has no representative in this country. His son was Richard Henderson, Town Clerk of Glasgow, who lived, as his father before him had done, in the tenement still standing at the south-west corner of Virginia Street."

We cannot forbear telling a good story of this Mr Henderson. He had a wooden leg, to which a dire misfortune one evening happened. He was a guest in a friend's house, which must have been old and rickety, for on Mr Henderson crossing the parlour floor, his wooden leg went through the rotten plank. A wag in the "flat" beneath, seeing the strange apparition, immediately seized upon it, and, fetching a saw, forthwith *severed the limb.* Poor Mr Henderson was assisted home, and for several days was unable to appear before "bench or bar;" and we can conceive that his first appearance with his new support must have tickled the risible faculties of his fellow citizens, who were never slow to relish a good joke.

On the death of the Rev. Mr Henderson, Blantyre can boast of having had "a disputed settlement," wherein the parishioners came off victorious, but only on the death of the unfortunate presentee. This was a Mr John Finnie, who had been licensed by the Presbytery of Glasgow, and was the librarian in the University. He was presented to Blantyre by David Erskine, Esq., W.S. (acting for the patron, Lord Blantyre), on the 8th of May, 1770. His settlement, as we have said, was opposed on account of bodily weakness and infirmity, the objectors declaring "he was more oppressed with the delivery of his sermons and discovered more symptoms of infirmity than their late pastor did at the time he was seized with the trouble of which he died." Undoubtedly the parishioners had too good a foundation for their objections, as Mr Finnie died towards the end of 1772. Although never admitted as a minister of Blantyre, we cannot withhold the following curious fact connected with his name: — During some time, when a licentiate, he was tutor in the family of Mr Matthew Orr of Stobcross, and he had the merit of suggesting to the proprietor of the soil the great advantages that would be derived from laying out and building a village adjoining to Anderston. That gentleman had the wisdom to act upon Mr Finnie's suggestions and plans, and built the village, which he called *Finnieston,* in honour of his humble but far-seeing tutor. Only the other day we passed by this quondam "village," now a gigantic suburb of Glasgow, and as we looked upon the noble docks crowded with some of the largest ships afloat, and listened to the ceaseless roar of the traffic, and the deafening clanging of the hammers beating into shape steamers that were destined for every land and clime on earth, we could not but whisper to ourselves — What a splendid monument is here to the name and memory of the "rejected presentee to Blantyre;" the feeble flame of whose life was no doubt quenched by the "disputed settlement."

For the gratification of the curious we subjoin here the names of the parishioners who were in favour of Mr Finnie, those who were against him, and those who prudently stood neutral in the contest. This list we found amongst papers kindly submitted for our perusal by Mrs Scott of Blantyre Farm : —

SMALL FEUARS.

For Mr Finnie. — Mr Boyes, Collector, Hamilton, Charles Barclay, John Donald, William Thomson, Alex. Pettigrew, William Watson, Archd. Watson, John Pollock.

Against Mr Finnie. — Charles Lyon in Hunthill, John Stevenson in Hunthill, James Eadie in Hunthill, Angus Sinclair in Hunthill, John Lyon in Barnhill, John Lyon, jr., in Barnhill, Robert Lyon in Barnhill, James Pettigrew in Barnhill, Robert Jackson in Pathfoot, James Dick in Pathfoot, Wm. Corbat in Causewaystanes.

Neutral. — James Stobs in Kirkton, Mary Mann there, John Cross in Blantyre Muir.

HEADS OF FAMILIES.

For Mr Finnie. — John Somerville in Aughhead, John Coats in Sydes, Thomas Dykes in Sydes, James Peatie in Aikentiber, John Bryson in Aikentiber, James Hamilton in Edge, James Warnock in Muir of Blantyre, James Lindsay in Park, John Littlejohn in Muir of Blantyre, James Millar in Sydes, James Craig in Aikenraith, Thos. Craig in Aikenraith, William Smellie in Shott.

Against Mr Finnie. — John Wilkie in Blantyre Farm, Matthew Morton in Blantyre Farm, Charles Weir in Barndykes Mill, William Coats in Woodhouse, Robert Jackson in Barnhill, John Burnlea in Barnhill, Robert Buchanan in Barnhill, John Cowper in Barnhill, John Liddel in Barnhill, Jas. Greenlees in Barnhill, Archd. Clark in Barnhill, James Smith in Barnhill, Matthew Liddel in Barnhill, John Thomson in Barnhill, Robert Connel in Millhaugh Mill, James Mann in Kirkton, James Skeelin in Kirkton, John Watson in Kirkton, William Fairsorvien in Kirkton, Jas. Martin in Kirkton, Robert Corbet in Kirkton, William Jackson in Hunthill, John Jackson in Burnhill, Jas. Cowper in Bellsfield, William Young in Calderside, James Young in Calderside, Gavin Lawson in Lucklayoch, Thos. Nimmo in Lucklayoch, John Lyon in Holmbarns, Gavin Lawson in Lodge Hill, Thos. Lawson in Sunnyside, Jas. Thomson in Park, Wm. Lusk in Aikenraith, Jean Wilson in Hunthill.

Neutral. — Jas. Cross in Blantyre Farm, Robt. Mackie in Barnhill, Alex. Brownlie in Barnhill, Jas. Hogg in Greenhead, Jas. Hamilton in Kirkton, Andrew Clark in Aikenraith, Jas. Clark in Aikenraith, Jas. Lusk in Aikenraith, Janet Brown in Barnhill, Jean Merrilies in Barnhill, Margt. Wilson in Barnhill, Margt. Dougall in Barnhill, Mary Craig in Barnhill, Jean Pollock in Hunthill, Mary Roger in Greenhead, Christian Pollock in Kirkton, Elizabeth Thomson in Kirkton, Marion Millar in Kirkton, Elizabeth Gray in Hunthill, Elizabeth Walker in Priestfield, Margaret Harvie in Priestfield, Janet Craig in Aikenraith, Christian Craig in Aikenraith, Margt. Jackson in Aikentiber.

Figure 3 Old Parish Church

VI.

There was a vacancy in Blantyre for about three years, but death having solved the difficulty between Mr Finnie and the parishioners, the patron presented the living to Mr Henry Stevenson, a native of Stewarton, and a licentiate of the Presbytery of Irvine. He was ordained on the 8th of May, 1773, and continued minister of Blantyre until his death, on the 27th December, 1808, in the seventieth year of his age, and thirty-sixth of his ministry.

Mr Stevenson married a Miss Muirhead, whose mother was a Portuguese lady. She has left to posterity a very candid opinion as to the merits of her son-in-law; for in broken English she was wont to affirm that "*Mr S. was no good at preach, but very good at game of cards.*" We are inclined to think that this foreign lady was a better judge about cards than the preaching, so we will accept her judgement with some hesitancy. Taken all over, Mr Stevenson was a most estimable man, and so were his three sons — Alexander and Henry, lately merchants in Glasgow, and Patrick, who went to push his fortune in Australia, and having done so successfully, returned to this country some years ago, and recently died at the Bridge-of-Allan.

Mr Stevenson, when minister of Blantyre, wrote a short but interesting history of the parish, which is to be seen in Sinclair's Statistical Account of Scotland, published in 1791. We have already alluded to it, and we will probably do so oftener ere we have done with our parish papers. He has likewise left behind him other monuments of his good work. Through his exertions in conducting a plea before the Court of Session, the stipend of the minister was considerably augmented; and it was no doubt from his persuasions that the heritors built the manse in 1773, which is still to the fore, and which is described in a gazetteer of the parish as being "*one of the prettiest manses in Scotland.*" A few years ago, an old general in India wrote to us a reminiscence of his early youth: how when he was a little boy, and a boarder with the minister of Mearns, he was driven over one beautiful summer's day, early in the present century, to pay a visit to the minister of Blantyre. Ever since there was imprinted in his mind a house, new fashioned then, situated in a paradise of flowers, and the air was redolent with the perfume of roses. There was evidently no *mining* in these days, and the parish dreamt not of coal pit chimneys and railway locomotives! Speaking of the manse, we may here state that in 1823 it was thoroughly repaired and a large addition made to it when occupied by the late Mr Lockhart, M.P., who had rented it whilst his own mansion house at Milton Lockhart was being rebuilt. For some years prior to his death, owing to the infirmities of age, Mr Stevenson had several assistants: one of whom was the Rev. Mr Fergus, father of Dr. Andrew Fergus, who is so well known amongst us as one of the most distinguished members of the Faculty of Physicians and Surgeons in the City of Glasgow Mr Stevenson's successor at Blantyre was the Rev. John Hodgson, son of the Rev. Joseph Hodgson, minister of Carmunnock. After being licensed by the Presbytery of Jedburgh, within whose bounds he was then residing as tutor at Milton Lodge (May, 1804), Mr Hodgson studied medicine in the University of Edinburgh, and graduated M.D., 1809. He was ordained at Blantyre on the 7th September, in the same year, and died very suddenly in Edinburgh on the 9th February, 1832, at the early age of fifty-two, having been minister of the parish twenty-two years.

There are several still living who can speak from personal recollection of the stately appearance of Dr. Hodgson, and of his manly eloquence as a preacher of the Gospel. Indeed, we have heard it affirmed that in the pulpit he was second only to Dr. Chalmers as a fervent and accomplished orator; and this testimony of him is certainly borne out by his two printed sermons which we have now before us. These are certainly of a wonderful length, but they likewise possess a wonderful power telling of the erudite scholar and the eloquent speaker. The one was preached before the Synod of Glasgow and Ayr in the year 1819; and the other is called "The Hamiltonian Sermon on the Advantages of the Reformation from Popery," preached in the Tron Church of Glasgow in the same year.

Here is a short quotation from the latter which we give as a specimen of his eloquence. He is advocating a grateful remembrance on the part of the people of Knox and the Reformers. *"We have read in our youth of patriot men, the avengers of a country's wrongs, and after witnessing, in severe experience, the meanness and selfishness of mankind, we turn again to the page of history with eagerness increased a thousandfold, and we trace, with a thrilling emotion, the sacred steps of Leonidas, of Wallace, or the archer, Tell; and a nation's gratitude bids the monument arise to perpetuate the memory of their deeds; of fetters broken and for ever cast away, of tyranny overthrown, of justice recalled from the heavens, and fixing her abode once more upon the earth. And shall no eye turn with eagerness to the page which tells of the mind emancipated; shall no heart throb with emotion, shall no breath breathe irregular as we read of those who burst the bands of spiritual slavery; who restored the reason to its freedom, and taught the man intellectual and at large, judging for himself, and aware of the responsibility to claim the place which belongs to him among the works of the Creator. I would bind the laurel on the patriot's brow; I would join with you my countrymen (if such your purpose be) in adding a stone to the heap which covers his remains, but while the fame of Wallace is to be preserved by an additional security, foul scorn I hold it, to be under the necessity of reminding you that no column has been raised to the memory of Knox, and that no church or edifice throughout the land which he delivered has been inscribed with his name."*

The sermon from which the above quotation is made, was preached soon after a meeting had been held in Glasgow with a view to erect a monument to the memory of Wallace — Henry Monteith, Esq., of Carstairs, Lord-Provost of the city, in the chair. And we may venture to suppose that this appeal of Mr Hodgson and others of a similar kind induced the worthy citizens to rear that monument to John Knox which now stands so prominent amidst the numerous marble statues in their beautiful Necropolis.

The sermon preached by Dr. Hodgson before the Synod of Glasgow and Ayr has the following glowing peroration, which might be read with profit by the people of this generation, as it reminds us *"how much we are indebted to the Fathers of the Scottish Church for our model system of national education"* : —

"There is a country of small geographical extent, whose shores have been pronounced inhospitable, whose sky has been described as ever foul with clouds, and whose surface is drenched with frequent rains; its produce is scanty, and its people have been represented as stretching out their hands to other nations for support.

"But to this country the eyes of Europe have been directed; assembled senates make choice of it as their best example, when in high debate, they resolve the question of the advantages of knowledge; and orators delight to expatiate upon it as the land of educated men.

"Do you know that country, my hearers? I am well persuaded that you distinguish its features, and rejoice in the proud peculiarity. Yes; and I am satisfied that there is not a mechanic, or a labourer among us, who would not deprive himself of the comforts, and even the necessaries, of life, in order to educate his children.

"And I offer thanksgiving to Almighty God, the Father of Mercies, that there is not an individual in our streets, whose face would not glow with the deepest blushes, were he to utter the language which the poet has put into the mouth of the peasantry in another part of the island —

> 'Approach thou and read, for thou can'st read the lay
>
> *(Thou* can'st read, but I *cannot)*
>
> Graved on the rock beneath yon aged thorn.'

Or if there be any individual to whom the name of Scotchman can be applied, so sunk in the infamy of hopeless degradation, as to utter without emotion such a sentiment as this, we own no tie of brotherhood, and claim no community with him.

"*Shall we, therefore, lightly esteem the men who have procured for us the high blessings of education? We revere their injured memory. Their names shall ever drop with sacred estimation from our lips; we will speak of their failings, if we speak of them at all, as a child would allude to the failings of a parent; we will dwell on their bright example, and, if we may indulge in such language, or entertain such a hope, we look forward to the time when we shall meet with them in the better country. Amen."*

During the incumbency of the last two mentioned ministers, Mr Stevenson and Dr. Hodgson, and even down to the year 1843, divine services were regularly conducted by ordained missionaries in the Chapel School in the village of Low Blantyre, their stipends being paid by Messrs. Henry Monteith & Co., the proprietors of the works. This was a great boon, as the distance from the Parish Church was too great to admit of many of the villagers being regular attendants. One of those missionaries was that eminent man of God, and most eloquent preacher, the late Rev. James Hamilton, who on leaving the Blantyre mission became minister of the High Church, Kilmarnock, where he laboured for a long time with great acceptance, and where he died at an advanced age but two years ago.

There were other two young evangelists who came after Mr

Hamilton, these were Mr Burn and Mr Duncan McLean. Many of the villagers still speak affectionately of these two ministers, and bear testimony to their worth and faithfulness. The last mentioned died of fever during his incumbency, and, at his own request, was buried in their little graveyard, beside the people he so much loved. The following inscription is on the tombstone —

"*Sacred to the memory of the Rev. Duncan McLean, preacher of the gospel, who died on the 13th February, MDCCCXLIV, having laboured nearly four years in his sacred calling with much acceptance among the people at Blantyre Works, by whom this tomb and tablet was erected.*"

VII.

The vacancy at Blantyre, caused by the sad and sudden death of Dr. Hodgson, in 1832, was filled up by the appointment of Mr James Anderson A.M., who was ordained to the living on the 13th September of the same year.

This gentleman was educated in the University of Edinburgh, where he took his degree, and was licensed by the Presbytery of Dunblane in the February of 1816. He was thus neither a young man nor a young preacher when he succeeded to Blantyre, which was his first charge; for Mr Anderson's "gifts" did not so much consist in pulpit oratory as in personal goodness and amiability. The universal tribute to his memory is this: that his was *"the meek and quiet spirit which in the sight of God is of great price."* The majority of his congregation differed from him in Ecclesiastical politics; but not one of them would deny him unqualified respect.

Only the other day an old woman said to us, in accents of tender affection: "*Oh, sir, if ever a pure Christian walked this earth it was Mr Anderson.*" He "*went out*" in 1843. "Having joined the Secession and signed the deed of Dismission, he was declared no longer a minister of this Church." Of his people, not a few went with him, to whom he continued to minister in holy things with his wonted fidelity and earnestness until he died on the 7th of May, 1860. In those gleanings of the past, which have given us so much pleasure, we would not, by a single word, hurt the feelings of any others who may not think as we do: but still we cannot but here record the unfeigned regret we feel on every remembrance of the lamentable secession of 1843. We give every meed of praise to those good and noble men, like Mr Anderson, who, for conscience sake, broke asunder the ties of deepest affection, and left the venerable Church of their fathers. But, to our mind, theirs was a mistaken and uncalled for sacrifice; for the objects they desired were to be fought for and gained, as they have been gained, by abiding in the Church, and not deserting it. What a blessed thing it would be to welcome a coming year that should prove itself the "healer of the breach," and when the two great sections, unhappily still apart, should let byegones be byegones, and heartily become as one, as they were of yore — a National Church, "beautiful for situation, the joy of the whole earth."

Mr Anderson was succeeded in the ministry of the Parish Church by Mr Samuel Paterson, a licentiate of the University of Glasgow, a man of undoubted abilities, and possessed of no mean qualifications as a preacher; indeed, he was considerably above the average. But, unfortunately, that we should be obliged to say it, the happiness of his life was destroyed, and its usefulness greatly marred, by unceasing domestic trials. He died in 1860. *De mortuis nil nisi bonum.* Strange coincidence, the two ministers in the parish, Mr Anderson and Mr Paterson, lay dead and unburied in their respective manses at the same time; and within a few hours they were both laid to sleep, side by side, in the old graveyard, and beneath the shadow of the church where they both had so often preached "the resurrection and the life."

It was a bright day for Blantyre when, in the month of October, 1860, the Rev. Paton James Gloag was inducted minister of the parish. We who have come after him can bear this honest and pleasant testimony, that, from the day of his induction to the day of his translation to Galashiels, he walked worthy of his high and holy vocation. An able scholar, a gifted preacher, a kindly friend, an unwearied Christian worker, he made himself felt through the length and breadth of the parish as a *power* for *good*. And this we testify, not so much to his praise; but, as he himself would have us do, to the praise and glory of the Divine Master, who ever moveth "amongst the candlesticks," and "holdeth the stars in His right hand, " and "without whom we can do nothing."

Mr Gloag was born in Perth, where his father was a banker; and by the Presbytery of his native city he was licensed in the month of April, 1846. In the September of the same year he was appointed assistant to the Rev. James Russell, D.D., of Dunning, and shortly afterwards ordained as "assistant and successor." He continued at Dunning for fourteen years, when he was translated to Blantyre. Here he remained for more than eleven years, when, much to the regret of his parishioners, he accepted the presentation to the parish of Galashiels, where he now abides. Mr Gloag deservedly received the honorary degree of Doctor of Divinity from the University of St. Andrews in March, 1867; for besides being an able and thoughtful preacher, he is justly held as being one of the foremost theological writers of the day. He has published many volumes on various subjects, all of which are very excellent.

Through the exertions of Dr. Gloag, our present beautiful Parish Church was erected just twenty years ago; and to him is greatly owing the erection of the still handsomer Parish Church of Galashiels, which is even now being completed to the admiration of all. Our review of Dr. Gloag's Ministry would certainly be deemed by many to be imperfect if no passing allusion was made to the unwearied and loving works of the amiable and gifted partner of his life. Full well has she proved herself "in sickness and in health" a true and faithful help-mate.

And here endeth our "role" of the "Blantyre Parish Ministers." Of course about ourselves we can say nothing. We must leave that onerous duty to some successor, who perhaps may deem it worth his while to rake up from oblivion our name and memory, but luckily for us, it shall be at a time when the voice of praise or blame can never reach us "*into the silent Land.*"

The present ecclesiastical state of the Parish is very different from what it was even in Dr. Gloag's time. Then the population was little over 3,000; now it is not far short of 10,000, with the prospect of a steady increase; then there were but two churches within its bounds, the Established Church, and a small Free Church; now the ecclesiastical edifices are numerous and varied. We have two large and handsome Parish Churches, a Free Church and Mission Hall, a beautiful church erected by the United Presbyterians, another of smaller dimensions belonging to the Evangelical Union denomination, and a Roman Catholic Church and School. Besides, are there not other "brethren" who meet in their respective halls, or who lift up their voices at the corners of our streets?

What a contrast is here, to the statistical record of fifty years ago; for this is the record. *"There is no dissenting chapel in the parish. Exclusive of the population at the Blantyre works, there are six families, including thirty individuals, belonging to the Relief, and two families, including seven individuals, belonging to the Roman Catholics. Divine service at the Parish Church is well attended."* Let us be glad, that with the increased demand for spiritual labourers, so many "have come over to help us;" and for them, as for ourselves, our honest prayer is that "the pleasure of the Lord may prosper in our hands."

Figure 4 New Parish Church

CHAPTER 2

Civil.

I.

About the time of the "War of Independence," the Barony of Blantyre appears to have belonged to the celebrated Thomas Randolph Earl of Moray, nephew of King Robert the Bruce — and one of the bravest of the brave, and foremost in that noble army of Scottish patriots.

Having made known this interesting fact, our readers will not be unwilling if we recall to memory one or two of the incidents in the life of this chivalrous hero, who, we are now proud to know, was once proprietor of Our parish. They will remember the prominent part he took in the battle of Bannockburn — as recorded in "The Tales of a Grandfather" — how the King posted Randolph, with a body of horse, near to the Church of St Ninians, commanding him to use the utmost diligence to prevent any succour from being thrown into Stirling Castle.

"After a short time, Bruce, who was looking out anxiously for the enemy, saw a body of English cavalry trying to get into Stirling from the eastward. This was the Lord Clifford, who, with a chosen body of 800 horse, had been detached to relieve the Castle. 'See, Randolph,' said the King to his nephew, 'there is a rose fallen from your chaplet.' By this he meant that Randolph had lost some honour by suffering the enemy to pass where he had been stationed to hinder him. Randolph made no reply, but rushed against Clifford with little more than half his number. The Scots were on foot. The English turned to charge them with their lances, and Randolph drew up his men in close order to receive the onset. He seemed to be in so much danger, that Douglas asked leave of the King to go and assist him. The King refused him permission. 'Let Randolph,' he said, 'redeem his own fault; I cannot break the order of battle for his sake.' Still the danger appeared greater, and the English horse seemed entirely to encompass the small handful of Scottish infantry. 'So please you,' said Douglas to the King, 'my heart will not suffer me to stand idle and see Randolph perish, I must go to his assistance.' He rode off accordingly, but long before they had reached the place of combat, they saw the English horses galloping off, many with empty saddles. 'Halt,' said Douglas to his men, 'Randolph has gained the day; since we were not soon enough to help him in the battle, do not let us lessen his glory by approaching the field.'

Now this was nobly done, especially as Douglas and Randolph were always contending which should rise highest in the good opinion of the King and the nation." On the death of King Robert, and during the minority of his son David, Randolph was Regent of the Kingdom, and a wise and just ruler he proved himself to be, so much so, that his death was regarded as a national calamity, and the grief of the people was so great, that it occasioned the historians to allege that he was poisoned by the English, but for this there seems to be no foundation. There is a pleasing story of this doughty Scottish chief, who would not brook the interference of English King or Romish Pope. "Upon one occasion, a criminal who had slain a priest, and afterwards fled to Rome, and done penance there, was brought before the Regent. The culprit confessed the murder, but pleaded that he had obtained the Pope's pardon. 'The Pope,' said Randolph, 'might pardon you for killing a priest, but his remission cannot avail you for murdering a subject of the King of Scotland;' and accordingly he caused the culprit to be executed. This was asserting a degree of independence of the Pope's authority, which was very unusual amongst the princes and governors of that time." So much for the first mentioned Laird of Blantyre.

Earl Randolph was succeeded by his two sons — Thomas and John — who became successively the second and third earls. They both died without issue, and their vast estates, in various parts of Scotland, including the Isle of Man, passed into the possession of their sister, the Countess of March — the celebrated "*Black Agnes of Dunbar.*"

During the national struggle for life and liberty, the Earl of March had acted an ignoble part, ever vacillating in his allegiance and attachment to his country's cause; but not so his wife: she inherited all the noble and patriotic spirit of her father. Our young readers would like to read the story of how she defended the Castle of Dunbar, so here it is :—

This castle was built upon a chain of rocks stretching out into the sea, and was of great strength. It was besieged for nineteen weeks by the Earls of Salisburgh and Arundel at the head of a large army, but the redoubtable lady defended it with great vigour. They used a large military engine which battered the walls with large stones, upon which the Countess and her maids would bend over the battlements and wipe the spots struck by those stones with a clean napkin: sneeringly intimating thereby that they could do no injury to the castle beyond raising a little dust which a napkin could wipe away. Again the besiegers employed another engine, which was called 'the sow,' as the roof of it resembled the ridge of a hog's back. It was rolled upon wheels close up to the walls, and beneath its sheltering roof the English soldiers worked with their pick-axes to effect an entrance through the wall. The Countess saw this engine advancing, and called out to the Earl of Salisburgh in derision, making rhyme with his name -

'Beware Montagow,
For farrow shall thy sow!'

Upon which she gave a signal, and a huge rock was hurled down upon the sow and broke its back. The English soldiers fled for their lives as arrows flew after them, and the Countess again shouted in derision — 'Behold the litter of English pigs!' Earl Salisburgh could not but admire the stern heroine who so successfully baffled all his attempts to take the castle. One night he rode near the wall with a knight dressed in armour of proof, having three folds of mail over an action or leather jacket. Notwithstanding which, one William Spence shot an arrow from the battlements with such force that it penetrated all these defences and reached the heart of the wearer. 'That is one of my lady's love tokens,' said the Earl as he saw the knight fall dead from his horse. 'Black Agnes's loveshafts pierce to the heart?' At length the siege ended. The Countess received supplies by sea both of men and provisions, and the English Earl, despairing of success, withdrew his forces. No wonder that the minstrels of the time sung aloud the praises of "Black Agnes," our Lady of Blantyre —

"She kept a stir in tower and trench,
The brawling, boisterous Scottish wench;
Came I early, came I late,
I found Agnes at the gate."

II.

Both the Earl and Countess of Dunbar died in the year 1369. It would appear that, a short time previous to their death, they made over the Baronies of Cumnock, in Ayrshire, and Blantyre, in Lanarkshire, to their son George, who afterwards succeeded to the Earldom. Here is the record of the deed of transference — "In 1368 King David II granted a charter to his cousin, George Dunbar, of the Baronies of Cumnock and Blantyre, with other lands, resigned by Patrick Dunbar, Earl of March, and his Countess."

This George, the 10th Earl, as all readers of history know well, became one of the most ambitious and powerful nobles of his time. He was the stern and fierce rival of the haughty Douglas. His daughter, Elizabeth, was betrothed to the unfortunate Duke of Rothesay, son of King Robert III, and heir to the throne, that prince, whose short dissipated life and whose melancholy death in the dungeon of Falkland Palace are so graphically told us by Sir Walter Scott in the "Fair Maid of Perth." Luckily for Elizabeth of Dunbar, her betrothal to the Prince was broken off. "The grim" Douglas protested against it, and through the influence of the infamous Duke of Albany, brother of the King, got the contract annulled, and secured the Prince for his own daughter Marjory. Their marriage took place in the year 1400, the nuptials being celebrated in the newly erected collegiate church of Bothwell — "It was an evil hour," truly says Sir Walter. Of course the proud Earl of March and Dunbar was indignant at the slight put upon him and his daughter by the breach of the contract of marriage, and so he renounced his allegiance, deserted the Scottish cause, and embraced that of England. To his lasting shame be it recorded that to gratify his own revengeful feelings he again and again ravaged with fire and sword the borderlands of his own country; and it was greatly through his help that Earl Percy, the celebrated "Hotspur," inflicted the disastrous defeat upon the Scottish army, under the Douglas, on the hill of Homildon.

Not very long afterwards this traitor Earl was reconciled to Douglas, and returned to Scotland. He died in 1420 at the age of 80. Many years before his death, he, like his mother before him, disponed to a kinsman the Baronies of Cumnock and Blantyre. This kinsman was David de Dunbar of Enterkin, whose descendants continued to be the proprietors for the next two centuries, till 1598, when the Barony of Blantyre was purchased from this family by Walter Stuart, commendator of Blantyre, to whom, as we have mentioned in a former paper, James VI had gifted the benefice and lands belonging to the Priory, and who was then created a Scottish Peer under the title of Lord Blantyre.

Not much, if any public interest, can be recorded of the Dunbars of Enterkin and Cumnock and Blantyre. The fullest printed information about them is contained in a privately printed pamphlet by the late Mr Sinclair regarding the Earldom of March, of which noble house they were a branch. Mr Burnett, Lyon King of Arms, has kindly furnished us with the following interesting item of intelligence — viz., "that an annual *reddendo* of a gold necklace or neck chain (monile aureum) from the Barony of Blantyre was, according to usual practice, doubled this year (1455) on entry of Patrick Dunbar heir to his father John Dunbar of Cumnock." And another mention of this "reddendo" is to be found at a much later date when one eighth of a necklace of gold of the weight of a Harry noble was paid for the lands of Birdsfield and Bellsfield in the Barony of Blantyre; the Barony having been, by this time, divided, and those lands forming one-eighth of the whole. We can throw no light whatever upon the origin of this particular tax of a gold necklace, but we may here mention that this and all other similar "reddendos" in those olden times were levied as a token of fealty to the Crown, and that the Lord of the Manor was bound, with his retainers, to join the King's forces in every time of war.

It is not our purpose, in those papers, to give a minute genealogical history of the noble family who take their name from our parish, and who have been in an unbroken line, the "superiors of the soil" for about 300 years. To do this would require more space than we can afford. We must, therefore, content ourselves with recording a few incidents connected with the Blantyre Family.

The first Lord Blantyre, Walter Stuart, was the son of Sir John Stuart of Minto, "Provost of Glasgow, and commandant of the castle of that town." He was educated along with King James VI by the famous historian, George Buchanan; and no doubt it was as a memento of their happy schooldays at "The Moss" in Dumbartonshire that he afterwards received from that monarch the

Priory of Blantyre. In many respects he was an eminent statesman, and did good service to his king and country.

In 1593 he was appointed an extraordinary Lord of Session, and soon afterwards was constituted one of the eight commissioners of the treasury and exchequer, called from their number "octavians," to whom King James entrusted the management of his affairs. Thereafter the office of High Treasurer was conferred upon him by letters patent, under the great seal, with a preamble very honourable to him. We find his name attached to the first "Protest" issued by "King James and his household and sundry others, to the glory of God, and good example of all men," against the usurped power of the Pope, and the manifold errors and corruptions of the Romish Church. This is a magnificent document. Our eyes rested on it for the first time a few days ago, when ransacking in an old library in the neighbourhood. No doubt the Lord High Treasurer had a goodly share in drawing up this protest, and well it testifies to the powerful intellects and large hearts of these stern old reformers. How refreshing to read of them coming down, like a sledge-hammer, upon the Pope's "cruel judgment against infants departing without the Sacrament of Baptism."

One day Lord Blantyre was riding up the street of Edinburgh, when he fell and broke his leg, and a courtier said, merrily, that it was no marvel the horse could not bear him "seeing he had so many offices ingrossed in his person." No doubt his lordship was a living testimony to the truthfulness of the proverb that — "In the light of the king's countenance is life, and his favour is as a cloud of the latter rain." But it is equally undoubted that Lord Blantyre was a man of exceptionally high character, and well merited the confidence his sovereign reposed in him and the exalted offices to which he had been raised.

Here is a little incident remotely connected with the first Lord Blantyre. All our readers have oftentimes looked at the two sides of a penny, but few of them know of any connection between the penny and the first Lord Blantyre; yet, curiously enough, there is. In the reign of that merry monarch, Charles II, there was a celebrated beauty at his court, whose name was Frances Theresa Stuart, and who was grand-daughter of the first Lord Blantyre. She is spoken of in the "Memoires de Grammont" as "la belle Stuart." The king became greatly enamoured with this lady, and that he might be at liberty to marry her, it is said that he entertained the design of getting divorced from his queen. This scheme, however, to his great indignation, was frustrated by Miss Stuart's privately marrying Charles, fourth Duke of Richmond and Lennox; a match promoted by Lord Clarendon to prevent the king carrying his purpose into effect. But though thus baffled, Charles was not vindictive. He continued his admiration of the Duchess, and paid her a strange compliment, in ordering that her face and figure should be perpetuated in the "Britannia" on our copper coins. So, please, take out your penny, and behold still engraven there the likeness of a once celebrated beautiful daughter of the house of Blantyre.

III.

In the middle of the old kirkyard there is still to be seen a little house, which is certainly not a thing of beauty; on the contrary, it is old and ugly and misshapen. Perhaps the builders of it thought that beauty would be out of place in such a house. Fortunately, opinions on this subject have materially changed; and men now seek to make their mausoleums and cemeteries as beautiful and attractive as can be. This little house of which we speak was the vault where the noble house of Blantyre were went to bury their dead. They are not buried here now, nor have been for more than a century: their burying-place having been transferred to Lennoxlove, a property possessed by the family in Haddingtonshire, and which had been bought by Alexander, fifth Lord Blantyre, with a portion of the large fortune bequeathed to him in 1702 by the beautiful Duchess of Richmond and Lennox. Hence the name given to the property, "Lennoxlove."

One of our first explorations after coming to the parish was to descend into this vault, guided by the old man, whose silvery hair we shall now see no more, and who had been forty years beadle and gravedigger. By the feeble light of a tallow candle we groped our way into the damp dark cell, the chilliness of which was somewhat terrible: and there we saw before us one long leaden coffin, only one, a solitary inmate of the dismal house. No doubt beneath the earth many other crumbled bodies lay. We asked the old man if he knew whose coffin this was? "No," was the reply; "but the tradition of the parish is that it contains the remains of a Lord Blantyre who was buried here some time in the last century. And with regard to the funeral," he continued, "I will tell you an incident. When I was a boy, over sixty years ago, I was told by an old man that he remembered well a bleak wintry day in his early boyhood, when the snow was lying thick upon the ground, and the storm was still raging — the school was just 'skailing,' — it was a wee bit place in that corner next to the manse — and the boys coming out saw a strange, unusual sight — a funeral, comprising a hearse with four horses and some mourning carriages, and they had the appearance of having had come a great distance. The procession stood before the gate, and a man hurrying up with a key opened the door of the vault, and a coffin was borne on the shoulders of stalwart men, whom the rest followed, down into the darkness, where they left their dead, and departed. They were all perfect strangers; silently they came and silently passed away. The people said that it was the body of a Lord Blantyre." And the people were right in their conjecture, for the leaden coffin contains the remains of William, ninth Lord Blantyre, who was a Colonel in the service of the States of Holland, and who died, unmarried, at Erskine, 16th January, 1776.

This Lord William was one of a family of six sons and four daughters. Three of the sons succeeded to the title, and the other three were more or less distinguished in the service of their country. One of them was a Lieutenant-Colonel in the army, and was killed at the battle of Guilford in North Carolina, on the 15th March, 1781; and another was an Indian Civilian, a member of the Supreme Council of Bengal, who is particularly mentioned in "Down's Narrative of the Campaign in India in 1792," as giving efficiency to the measures of Lord Cornwallis in his successful conflict against Tippo Sahib in the Mysore.

The eldest of the three brothers who successively became barons, was Walter, who resided much on the Continent, and died at Paris in the 26th year of his age on the 21st May, 1751. He was buried at Blantyre. Contemporary writers speak of him as a young nobleman of great promise, accomplished manners, and amiable character. Here is an interesting, albeit not very grammatical, extract from a letter written by Lady Jane Hamilton, the Defendant and successful Litigant in the famous Douglas Peerage Case. It is dated, Utrecht, 10th February, 1747 — "Among the rest of the British, young Lord Blantyre deserves the greatest praise. He has extreme good sense; the best scholar, the greatest application, a vast pleasure in reading, and the best taste of books; is free from all manner of vice, and has the sweetest temper in the world, and in all appearance will be a very great honour to his country." And in the *Scots Magazine* of the year of his death there are two poetical tributes to the memory of this noble youth. We make the following quotation from one of them :—

Nor shall domestic tears alone deplore
A loss that ring's o'er weeping Gallia's shore,
Where Blantyre's name shall never be forgot,
Where Peers and Princes mourn their Darling Scot.

Mourn him, ye muses, he so dearly loved,
Mourn him, ye graces, by whose aid he moved,
Mourn him, ye wise, who to his praise aspire,
Mourn him, ye fools, who now too late admire,

Mourn him, ye young, improve from what you've seen,
Mourn him, ye aged, think what he'd have been.
Yes all must mourn, though no one may repine
A sun which set when just begun to shine.

Ye partner objects of a pious care,
The justest joy with justest sorrow share,
Nor deem your ever dearest brother lost,
For general good, good heaven your wishes crossed.

To teach mankind, what oft is taught in vain,
That human hopes have but a moment's reign,
That bloom and beauty, parts and pomp and power
Are but the flashes of a fleeting hour;

To teach mankind the improvement of its span,
The only praise, the only pride of man;
To enforce a lesson little understood
That to be great is only to be good.

We wonder if our Poet Laureate ever came in contact with this eulogy to help him a little to his beautiful stanza —

"Howe'er it be, it seems to me,
'Tis only noble to be good,
Kind hearts are more than coronets
And simple faith than Norman blood."

On the death of Lord William, his brother Alexander succeeded to the title. It was he who first resided at Erskine House, an old mansion situated near the Clyde in Renfrewshire, and which he made the principal seat of the family. This nobleman, like his much lamented brother, was a most estimable man, and devoted himself entirely to the interests of his tenantry and the improvement of his property. Indeed, the rich fields of Erskine testify to this day to "his accurate and extensive knowledge of the principles of agriculture."

In the statistical account of the parish, written an hundred years ago, immediately after the death of Lord Blantyre, we find the following tribute to his worth:— *"The writer of this account feels a particular satisfaction in having an opportunity of exhibiting such an example, and at the same time paying a deserved tribute to the memory of an amiable and respectable nobleman and a most worthy and useful citizen, whose death was lamented by the people of all ranks in this county as a public misfortune. His conduct as a landlord was not only humane but highly judicious, as it equally tended to promote the real interest of proprietor and tenant, and the general advantages of the country."* He died at Clifton on the 5th November, 1783.

IV.

None who went with us in June last will forget the bright happy day they spent in the grounds of Erskine. Having received the kind permission of Lord Blantyre to hold our midsummer fete in a field adjoining his mansion, we journeyed with railway speed to Bishopton, thence we marched with banners flying and to the national music of the bagpipes, through the beautiful policies and gardens and terraces until we came to the field of our festivities. And what a view from that gently sloping field there was — one of the finest in all Scotland. There at our feet, just widening into the noble Firth, flowed the majestic river, over whose calm and sunlit waters, sailed unceasingly ships of every size and diverse form; and on the opposite shore arose, like a solitary sentinel, the rock and castle of Dumbarton, with their thousand memories illustrative of noble deeds in Scottish history; whilst beyond there jutted forth into the Firth the wooded promontory of Roseneath, and still farther away, piercing the blue sky, were the peaked mountains of Argyllshire. It was a scene, viewed from that hill at Erskine, that would kindle the heart of the veriest dotard into enthusiasm.

But not only did the natural beauties of the scenery attract our attention on that bright summer day, there was an object that rose near to us, which we could not but look upon with a melancholy interest. It was an obelisk monument of freestone, bearing the following inscription :—

"ERECTED BY THE COUNTY OF RENFREW
To THE MEMORY OF THE RIGHT HONOURABLE
ROBERT WALTER, 11TH LORD BLANTYRE,
A Major-General in the British Army,
and formerly Lord Lieutenant of Renfrewshire,
in testimony of respect for his public services,
and as a tribute of esteem for his private worth.
Died, 23rd September, 1830."

This noble peer, whose melancholy death is here recorded, for he was accidentally shot at Brussels, was son of the famous agriculturist, and father of the present peer. He had been a distinguished soldier, and passed through the dangers of many a bloody battlefield. His military career commenced with the disastrous expedition into Holland under the Duke of York, when the humiliating spectacle was presented to the world of a British army, through incompetent generalship, capitulating to an enemy. A universal wail was raised then, even as it is sometimes now, over the degeneracy of the British soldiery, and that henceforth and for ever they had declined from their former renown. But very soon Lord Blantyre and his fellow-soldiers had the opportunity of proving what stuff they were made of, for the time was at hand, as the historian relates, "when a greater commander, wielding the resources of a more courageous and excited nation was to wash out these stains on British Arms, and show to the astonished world that England was yet destined to take the lead, even on the Continent, in the deliverance of Europe, and that the blood of the victors of Poictiers and Blenheim yet flowed in the veins of their descendants."

Two years after this Dutch humiliation, Lord Blantyre, as aide-de-camp to General Stewart, accompanied the army to Egypt in pursuit of the legions of France, and no doubt he was amongst the blue bonnets of the gallant 42nd when, with their brave comrades of other regiments, they stormed the sandy heights of Aboukir, and on the field of Alexandria fought for the empire of the East and won it, wrenching from the hitherto conquering French their boastful title of "Invincibles." The charm which had paralysed the world was then broken, and on the standards taken by the victors, they pointed with exultation to the names — "Le Passage de la Scrivia," "Le Passage de Tagliamento," "Le Passage de I'Isonza," "La Prize de Gratz," "Le Pont de Lodi."

Returning from Egypt, Lord Blantyre next saw service in the Expeditions to Copenhagen and Holland and in the Peninsula. For several years he commanded the Second Battalion of the 42nd Regiment (the Black Watch) during the campaigns in Portugal and Spain under the Duke of Wellington. And so the history of that distinguished regiment at that stirring and eventful time was the history of the military career of Lord Blantyre. In St Giles Cathedral in Edinburgh, now so beautifully restored to its pristine grandeur, are to be seen those most interesting relics of a stormy past, many of the old colours of our Scottish Regiments. Among them is one with a few tattered rags attached to the staff, telling woefully of "the battle and the breeze;" and around the staff will be read a long list of names, among them being — Egypt, Corunna, Fuentis D'Onor, Pyrenees, Nivelle, Nive, Orthes, Toulouse, Peninsula, etc. These were the battles in which the 42nd took part when Lord Blantyre was connected with it. After the battle of Fuentis D'Onor, he was honourably mentioned in Lord Wellington's despatch as having repulsed a regiment of cavalry that had broken in upon the British infantry. And to show the sense which the Commander-in-Chief had of Lord Blantyre's merits, we may state that a public order of thanks of the most flattering kind was issued to him and his regiment on his leaving the Peninsula. General Stewart, who was then likewise an officer in the Black Watch, tells us in his graphic history that during the short interval of peace from the close of the Peninsular war to the Waterloo campaign, he made a journey into France and met some of the French officers who had so stubbornly opposed the advance of the British troops through the defiles of the Pyrenees. It will not be unpleasant to Scottish ears to hear what those brave opponents had to say of the Highlanders of those days :—

"I was travelling through Languedoc, and in a field close to the road near to Carceson I saw a brigade of French Infantry exercising. Stepping out of the carriage, I walked into the field to view the troops, and being in uniform I was observed by the general officer commanding. He immediately rode up, and after the usual salutations, invited me with great politeness to look at his brigade; and, opening the ranks, we walked through each rank together. In the course of conversation the recent battles were noticed, and after discussing various points; 'Well,' said the French General, 'we are quite satisfied if the English army think we have fought bravely, and done our duty well.' The Highland corps were mentioned. 'Ah,' said he, 'these are brave soldiers. I would not like to meet them again unless I was well supported. I put them to the proof that day' — alluding to the battle of Toulouse, the last one fought. I asked him in what manner. He said that he led the division which attempted to retake the redoubt which had been taken and held by the Black Watch. And on a further question as to the strength of that division, 'More than 5000 men,' was the answer. Thus those thousands were repulsed, with great slaughter, by the 42nd, supported by the 91st. The Highlanders also suffered very severely. The French General had good reason to extol the bravery of the soldiers "sans culotte."

At the close of the Peninsular Campaign, which all the world then thought would have been the termination of the European struggle, Lord Blantyre retired from the army and spent the remaining years of his life principally at his estate of Erskine. He built the present handsome mansion house, but which he was not destined to see finished. The manner of his death is thus shortly told by his son in a letter which his lordship has kindly sent to us. "My father had taken a house at Brussels, and was residing there with his family — a corner house of the principal square — when the Belgians rose against the Dutch. There was skirmishing in the square. About 7 a.m. my father, while dressing, looked out of a window, when a shot pierced his neck. He never spoke again, being choked with blood. It was never known whether the shot was a stray shot or fired purposely at one who might be at the window as a sharpshooter — it was likely quite an accident." So fell a brave man. He was succeeded in the peerage by his second son, Charles Walter, the present Lord Blantyre.

Since writing the above we have received from the present peer an obituary notice of his father which appeared in the *Spectator,* 1830, immediately after his death. We give the following extract from it:—

"In addition to his claims as a public character, this lamented nobleman was highly distinguished for the virtues of private life. His affectionate and exemplary conduct as a son, a brother, a husband and a father, the excellence of his character founded on religious principle, and the warm sensibilities of his heart, united as they were in him with a peculiar elegance and sweetness of manner — and his delicate attentions to everyone, but chiefly to those who needed most to be encouraged and brought into notice, endeared him to his relatives and friends, and made him an object of respect wherever he was known. In 1813, soon after his return from Spain, he married an amiable young lady, the grand-daughter of the late Admiral Lord Rodney, with whom he continued to live in a state of the greatest comfort and happiness, and by whom he had an interesting family of nine children, the youngest, twins, being born only three months before his untimely death. Having paid a visit to Scotland as soon as he could after the birth of those infants (the object of which was chiefly to accelerate the finishing of his new and elegant mansion at Erskine on the Clyde, with a view to his taking up his residence in it next summer), he had passed to Brussels as the Dutch troops were approaching it, and found himself again in the bosom of his family who, as may well be supposed at the time of general alarm, received him with the most cordial welcome, and clung to him as their guardian angel. But, alas! on the morning of the 23rd of Sept. having gone to a window in an upper room of the house, and at a time when no danger was apprehended, to look out for an instant on the Dutch troops who were advancing through the Rue Royale in the Park, he was struck on the neck by a musket-ball fired obliquely from the corner of the park, which divided the carotid artery, and by the effusion of blood which it caused deprived him almost instantly of his life."

V.

When the first Lord Blantyre purchased the barony of Blantyre, in 1598, from the Dunbars of Enterkin, he must have found the parish, to a great extent, divided into perpetual feus; and as more feus were granted, without any reservation, by his immediate successors, the whole land became honey-combed as regards proprietorship.

A hundred years ago, our predecessor, Mr Stevenson, says: *"There are at present 37 heritors who pay cess; and of these 10 do not reside in the parish. The landed property has very seldom been transferred; for, though there are few possessed of more than a plowgate of land, and some who have only a few acres, yet many of these small possessions have been inherited by the same family for some hundred years. This retention of landed property is plainly to be imputed to the industry, frugality, and amiable rural simplicity of the inhabitants. The whole parish consists of 24 plowgates of land, each plowgate containing about 80 acres; and, for the most part, the proprietor occupies his own land."*

These remarks are, to some extent, applicable to matters as they now are: there are about the same number of heritors; but the last hundred years have seen various transferences of property, and few of the present proprietors have inherited their possessions from the time when Lord Blantyre bought the barony. We have a curious old document now before us. It is the record of a summons raised in 1635 by the heritors of Blantyre against *"Lord Blantyre, titular, and Mr John Heriot, minister of the parish,"* on a disputed point regarding "Parsonage Teinds." A few in this old list of heritors are represented at the present day: such as the Hamiltons of Blantyre Farm, by Mrs Scott; the Jacksons of Barnhill and Bardykes, by the families of the same name; the Clarks of Auchinraith, by Mr John Clark Forrest; and the Craigs, in the same locality, by the families of that name who have now got the properties of Birdsfield and Burnbrae. There were other heritors, at that distant period, whose names are not in the list alluded to, but whose direct descendants are still in possession of the lands. These are the Millars of Milheugh, the Maxwells of Shott, and the Wardropes of Greenhall; and, though not dating so far back, the lands of several other proprietors have been in the possession of their families for several generations.

The Hamiltons of Borland and Blantyre Farm were a very old and honourable family, able to trace their direct descent from the ancient house of Hamilton of Cadzow (Walter Fitz-Gilbert), who was really the founder of the "clan," if we may dare to call them so. George, the second son of Sir David Hamilton of Cadzow, and grandson of the above mentioned Walter Fitz-Gilbert, the first of that ilk, bought the estate of Borland, in the parish of Cumnock, in Ayrshire, from the Dunbars of Enterkin, in the year 1400; and his son Thomas purchased from the same family the property of Blantyre Farm, or, as it was then called, "Fremblantyre." This was about the year 1452. Twenty years afterwards we find recorded an instrument of sasine "to William Hamilton, son and heir of Thomas Hamilton, quondam of Fremblantyre, of the lands of West Barn, in the constabulary of Haddington, from George, Lord Seton, 26th April, 1475." Evidently this branch of the Hamilton family had a considerable craving after land. We cannot minutely follow their genealogical history, although their "tree," with its many branches, is now before us; but this we must say, that for many generations, and even centuries, they occupied a prominent and honourable position in the barony of Blantyre. From 1681 to 1752, James and Alexander Hamilton, father and son, were successively "baron baillie" and factor to Lord Blantyre; and not only managed his Lordship's property in this parish, but likewise the other estates of Erskine, Kilpatrick, Dunottar, and Cardonald. The baillie must have wielded a considerable amount of power in those days, for we find, from a paper with his own handwriting, that on the 18th May, 1709, Mr James Hamilton, as "the baillie, fynes ilk ane of the vassals in fyve pounds Scots for not having payd their rent on that day," and here follows a long list of the delinquents. We will not publish their names, but where could the lairds have been?

The Millars of Milheugh are likewise a very old Blantyre family. Their original grant of land was obtained from the Dunbars of Enterkin, some time in the fifteenth century, and in 1602 a fresh title was got from Walter, Lord Blantyre. The "Mylnes" must have been a very profitable possession, for we find from an old paper that, as early as the year 1564, John Myllar of Mylneheugh had money to invest, and bought a ground rent from the laird of Calderwode; but this possession Mr Myllar bound himself to restore "upon receiving payment of one hundred pundis Scotts any day, betwixt the sun rising and going down, within the parish kirk of Blantyre." The Christian name of John seems to have been held in high repute by this family, for out of nine proprietors, no fewer than seven were John Millars, and the present heir to the property is Colonel John Millar Bannatyne. We will anon devote a few pages to the life and writings of Professor John Millar, of the University of Glasgow, who was certainly one of our "Eminent Men."

All the "Lairds" of Blantyre pay feu-duty to Lord Blantyre as Superior of the Soil: this consists invariably of a small sum of money. There is one curious exception. The proprietor of Bardykes holds his land on the condition that when required he must present a red rose to the Lord of the Barony. Well (good) for him that he has got a greenhouse! We cannot trace the origin of this strange feu-duty. Bardykes came into possession of the family of the Jacksons in the year 1525, for in an old paper before us there is mention made of "an chartour granted by Robert Dalziel of Rylandside, with the consent of John Stuart of Halrighs, curators for the lands of John Dunbar of Blantyre, to John Jackson and Janet Miller his spouse, to them two, of the west half of Bardykes, to be holden of the said Robert Dalziel in *feudo et hereditate,* dated the 25th of October, 1525: Item an precept of seasine granted by John Dunbar of Blantyre for infefting of the said John Jackson, younger, and Janet Miller his spouse, in the twenty shilling land of the old extent of Bardykes called the west half, dated the 28th of June, 1532."

If those original papers are anywhere in existence, they might throw some light upon this mysterious "red rose." We know of a gentleman who holds his property in Argyllshire on the condition that he will be always ready to ferry Royalty across the river Awe whenever a King or a Queen of Scotland, or a member of the Royal Family, comes to demand his services. They have never come as yet; but, like a wise man, his motto is "ready, aye ready." And everyone knows the story of John Howison, how, as a reward for the timely help he gave to the goodman of Ballangeich when fighting with the gipsies, he received from the King the farm of Braehead, on which he was a bondsman; but on the condition that John Howison or his successors should be ready to present an ewer and basin for the King to wash his hands when his Majesty should come to Holyrood Palace, or should pass the bridge of Cramond. *"Accordingly,"* says Sir

Walter Scott, "*in the year 1822, when George IV came to Scotland, the descendant of John Howison of Braehead, who still possesses the estate which was given to his ancestor, appeared at a solemn festival and offered his Majesty water from a silver ewer, that he might perform the services for which he held his lands.*" Thus there may be throughout Scotland many strange feu-duties — curious conditions on which property was originally attained, and is now held.

Apropos to the above, we find that Mr George Augustus Sala in his last "Echoes of the Week" tells the following incident connected with the origin of the word "D'Oyley":— "*William the Conqueror created his friend and follower, Robert D'Oyley, Baron Hocknorton (A.D. 1067), granting him the city and barony of Oxford, and twenty-eight lordships in that county. He also held the manor of Pushall Nappa of the crown in capitè by sergeantcy by the yearly tendor of a table cloth of three shillings value at the feast of St Michael. Agreeably to the fashion of the time, the ladies of the D'Oyley family were accustomed to embroider and ornament the quit-rent tablecloths, hence these little cloths became curiosities, and accumulating in the course of years were at length brought into use as napkins at the royal table. Record is extant of a suit brought in Hilary-term (12th Edward) by the Attorney-General on behalf of the crown against the feudatory owner of Pushall Nappa for the tablecloth.*"

CHAPTER 3

Eminent Men

I — PROFESSOR JOHN MILLAR OF MILLHEUGH.

"*JOHN MILLAR, Professor of Law, in the University of Glasgow, was born on the 22nd June, 1735, in the parish of Shotts, twenty-four miles west from Edinburgh. His father, Mr James Millar, a man much respected for his abilities, learning, and purity of manners, was then minister of that parish; but two years afterwards he was translated to Hamilton, where he spent the rest of his life. His mother was a daughter of Mr Hamilton of Westburn, a gentleman of considerable estate in the county of Lanark.*

When the family removed to Hamilton, Mr Millar went to reside at Milheugh, in the parish of Blantyre, eight miles from Glasgow, with his uncle, Mr John Millar, who had been educated in Edinburgh as a Writer to the Signet, but from bad health had given up that profession, and retired to a small estate which had been long in his family."

But although Professor Millar was not thus born in our parish, he was in every respect a Blantyre man, as his ancestors had been in possession of Milheugh for centuries, as already stated, and on the death of his uncle in 1785, he himself became the proprietor, and there he lived many happy years with his numerous family until the close of his life in 1801. Here is a very pretty description of the Professor's house and its environs, as given by Mr Craig, his biographer. It will give our readers who may be strangers to our parish an idea of some of the "warm retreats" in Blantyre:— "*Milheugh possesses many natural beauties. It consists of several small meadows separated from each other by the Calder, a little stream which winds among them, sometimes skirting, at other times intersecting the valley. The bushes which fringe the edges of the rivulet, and a number of large trees standing near the house, and shading some of its principal walks, give great richness to the scene, while the steep banks which rise from each side of the valley suggest ideas of retirement and seclusion. But when Mr Millar came to Milheugh there was much to alter and improve.*

He removed many formal hedges which sub-divided the little meadows, or by stiff unbending lines marked too distinctly the course of the rivulet. He formed the old orchard into pleasing groups of trees around the house, left bushes irregularly scattered on the banks of the stream, and carried plantations along the top of the banks. Everything throve in this sheltered situation, and Milheugh is now one of the sweetest retirements that could be desired. Its beauties are elegant and simple, and perhaps it would be difficult to point out any further embellishments that would accord with the character of the place."

Few of the present generation have ever heard of the name of Professor John Millar, and fewer still know anything whatever about his life and teachings; and yet in his day — and Scotland had then many great thinkers — we question if any of them were superior to Mr Millar in scholarship, in literary knowledge, in originality and power of intellect, — and none of them exercised a wider and more beneficial influence over the minds of the many aspiring youths who flocked to his class-room in the Glasgow University during the long period of forty years.

James Watt, of undying fame, thus writes of him as he was in early life — "In our meetings the conversation, besides the usual subjects with young men, turned principally on literature, religion, morality, history — and to these conversations my mind owed its first bias to such subjects. Mr Millar was always looked up to as the oracle of the company — his attainments were greater than those of the others — he had more wit and much greater argumentative powers. He was a man when I was a boy, although in years little my senior. The diversity of our pursuits made me know less of him afterwards than I should otherwise have done, but we always continued attached friends, and I consider myself as indebted to him for much useful knowledge."

And here is a splendid testimony to the influence of Professor Millar's lectures. We extract it from a recent number of the *Edinburgh Review* upon the "Letters and Discoveries of Sir Charles Bell," — "But the three men who more than any others determined their future course were John Millar, John Playfair, and Dugald Stewart. John Millar was professor of Law in Glasgow University — a lecturer of immense range and power of expression, and with that magnetic influence, which seemed an instinct, of attracting, warning, and charming the enthusiasm of youth. In vain did the exacting spirit of conformity to the tenets in vogue brood over Scotland, — while, session after session, to fresh relays of delighted listeners, John Millar's eloquence fixed deeply into their minds the principles of free constitutional government. His class thus became a great training school for the lawyers and statesmen of the next generation, and many of them in after life owned that Millar's prelections had first given the impulse which stimulated them throughout life. It is said that both Jeffrey and Brougham were his pupils. Lord Melbourne, Lord Lauderdale, Lord Moncrieff, and many others, certainly were so; but there can be no question that the bold lines of thought on which the *Edinburgh Review* was afterwards constructed were first laid down by his masterly hand."

It can scarcely be credited in our day that Mr Millar was the first Professor of Law in Scotland who delivered his lectures in the English language. True, indeed, his immediate predecessor, was bold enough to use the English in a series of lectures he delivered on the "Institutes of Justinian," but the Faculty of Advocates were so shocked at this daring innovation that they made formal application to the University, requesting that the practice of teaching the civil law in Latin might be restored.

Of course they could not make the shadow of the sun go back upon the dial. From the day of his appointment to the Chair, Mr Millar adopted the English language in all the courses of lectures which he delivered. No doubt this common-sense movement helped greatly to increase his popularity and drew to his class-room young men from Edinburgh and other places. For had the law professors in Edinburgh introduced the same change it might have greatly interfered with the Glasgow professor's success, but they continued for a long time to read their lectures in Latin, and before they thought proper to abandon this custom Mr Millar's fame was too well established and too widely diffused to admit of any competition.

Professor Millar was an innovator in another way, but for this innovation we of a later generation are not grateful to him — he never wrote his lectures. "*He was accustomed to speak from notes, containing his arrangement, his chief topics, and some of his principal facts and illustrations. He trusted to that extemporaneous eloquence which seldom fails a speaker deeply interested in his subject.*" This certainly was to the great benefit of them who heard the living voice, but it is an irreparable loss to us who have come after: the lectures are gone with the speaker except in so far as they live in the thoughts and teachings of others. From all descriptions Professor Millar must have been, as a lecturer — and perhaps too, in his athletic form — very much like Professor Wilson of Edinburgh, the famous Christopher North, who as a boy, when boarding with Professor Jardine at Hallside, was a frequent guest at Milheugh. And him we can remember well: it was a vision worth living for to see ;— that old erect stalwart man, with his gown hanging carelessly over his arms, and his yet golden locks curling down upon his brawny shoulders, and his whole frame quivering with emotion, — and his eagle eye flashing with excitement, — and his voice sending forth a torrent of eloquence upon the silent sea of upturned youthful faces. Suddenly the voice would be hushed, the great hand gathered up the sibylline leaves and crumpled them together, and amongst vociferous cheering "the Professor" passed away. Truly these extemporaneous lecturers are grand in their eloquence, and produce a lasting influence for good upon their audience, but the world loses much from their unwritten thoughts.

The only two works by Professor Millar which have been published and bequeathed to posterity are "The Origin of the Distinction of Ranks," and an "Historical View of the English Government." In telling us that this latter book was written entirely in the country during the summer recess, the biographer gives us a glimpse into the Professor's happy home at Milheugh:— *"While carrying on this last work, it very frequently became the subject of conversation in the family, and all the opinions and speculations it contained were freely canvassed. He had long been in the habit of consulting Mrs Millar with regard to his literary works; and some of his children being, by this time, competent judges of composition, he occasionally read over to his family the most amusing or interesting passages, and listened with much attention to their various criticisms. By this means, besides increasing that mutual confidence which ever subsisted between him and his family, he had the means of detecting any little errors which had escaped his own observation, and he formed the taste while he improved the judgment of his children."*

We give here two extracts from Professor Millar's work on the "Origin of the Distinction of Ranks," that our readers may judge for themselves of the purity and elegance of his diction, and the originality and power of his thoughts. The first is on *The origin of a chief.* "Superiority in strength, courage, and other personal accomplishments, is the first circumstance by which any single person is raised to be the leader of a tribe, and by which he is enabled to maintain his authority. In that rude period, when men live by hunting and fishing, they have no opportunity of acquiring any considerable property; and there are no distinctions in the rank of individuals, but those which arise from their personal qualities, either of mind or body.

The strongest man in a village, the man who excels in running, in wrestling, or in handling those weapons which are made use of in war, is, in every contest, possessed of an evident advantage which cannot fail to render him conspicuous, and to command respect and deference. In their games and exercises, being generally victorious, he gains an ascendancy over his companions, which disposes them to yield him pre-eminence, and to rest fully satisfied of his superior abilities. When they go out to battle, he is placed at their head, and permitted to occupy that station where his behaviour is most likely to be distinguished and applauded. His exploits and feats of activity are regarded by his followers with pleasure and admiration; and he becomes their boast and champion in every strife or competition with their neighbours. The more they have been accustomed to follow his banner, they contract a stronger attachment to his person, are more afraid of incurring his displeasure, and discover more readiness to execute those measures which he thinks proper to suggest. Instead of being mortified by his greatness, they imagine that it reflects honour upon the society to which he belongs, and are even disposed to magnify his prowess with that fond partiality which they entertain in favour of themselves.

In many savage tribes, the captain of an expedition is commonly chosen from the number of wounds he has received in battle. The Indians of Chili are said, in the choice of a leader, to regard only his superior strength, and to determine this of another. The introduction of personal liberty has therefore an infallible tendency to render the inhabitants of a country more industrious; and, by producing greater plenty of provisions, must necessarily increase the populousness, as well as the strength and security of a nation.

But slavery is not more hurtful to the industry than to the good morals of a people. To cast a man out from the privileges of society, and to mark his condition with infamy, is to deprive him of the most powerful incitements to virtue; and, very often, to render him worthy of that contempt with which he is treated. What effects, on the other hand, may we not expect that this debasement of the servants will produce on the temper and disposition of the master? In how many different ways is it possible to abuse that absolute power with which he is invested? And what vicious habits may be contracted by a train of such abuses, unrestrained by the laws, and palliated by the influence of example? It would seem that nothing could exceed the dishonesty and profligacy of the Roman slaves, unless we except the inhumanity and the extravagant vices which prevailed among the rest of the inhabitants.

Considering the many advantages which a country derives from the freedom of the labouring people, it is to be regretted that any species of slavery should still remain in the dominions of Great Britain, in which liberty is generally so well understood, and so highly valued."

II. — DAVID LIVINGSTONE.

Once, but only once, were we in the society of David Livingstone. It was in the house of our mutual friend, Mr Hannan, of Messrs Henry Monteith, & Co., over twenty years ago. We were under orders for India, and he was about to start on his second expedition to Africa. There are sunny spots in a man's memory, and such is the hour of conversation we then had with Livingstone. It could scarcely be called a conversation, for *he* talked and *we* listened; and never can we forget the eagle eye, the fervid talk, the warm, loving heart, the self-abnegating spirit, the nobleness of the gentleman.

We knew nothing of Blantyre in those days, much less could we dream that the future lot should be ours to be minister of this parish where the great traveller was born and bred. — Yes, in a little room, up a spiral stair, in a three storied block of buildings at the Blantyre Mills, he was born, and in the village school he received his early education under the instructions of that master of whom he afterwards wrote so gratefully as being so kind and attentive and so skilled in tuition that many of his pupils attained to positions in after life far above what they ever appeared likely to come to in the village school. And it is interesting to note how in those early years, as the apprentice lad in Blantyre Works, Livingstone gave evidence of the true old adage, "*That the boy is the father of the man;*" for as a boy he had great difficulties to encounter ere he attained the object of his ambition — viz., to educate and elevate himself for nobler walks and higher things; but these difficulties he met and triumphed over them; — even so when a man, he had set his heart upon the grand two-fold object — To open up the African continent, and deliver its millions from the curse of slavery and heathenism; and as we well know, from that object no difficulties, the most terrible, could make him for one moment swerve. This tenacity of purpose so early displayed by the youthful piecer, how conspicuous was it in the veteran traveller.

Stanley, the last white man who saw him alive, thus writes of him:— *"The sport of adverse circumstances, the plaything of the most miserable beings sent to him from Zanzibar, he has been baffled and worried down even to the grave — yet he will not desert the charge imposed upon him. To the stern dictates of duty alone he has sacrificed his home and ease, the pleasures, the refinements, and luxuries of civilized live. His is the Spartan heroism, the inflexibility of the Roman, the enduring resolution of the Anglo-Saxon — never to relinquish his work, though his heart yearns for home; never to relinquish his obligations until he can write finis to that work."*

But to return to his youth. Here is a fine picture for the pencil of some young Scottish painter. *"My reading, while at work, was carried on by placing the book on a portion of the spinning jenny, so that I could catch sentence after sentence as I passed at my work. I thus kept up a pretty constant study, undisturbed by the roar of the machinery. To this part of my education I owe my present power of completely abstracting the mind from surrounding noises, so as to read and write with perfect comfort amidst the play of children, or near the dancing and songs of savages."* Livingstone left *"the sweet and pretty village of Blantyre"* — that is what *he* calls it — to continue his studies in Glasgow University, for in those days there was but a step from the lowly parish school to the lofty city college. In due time, he finished the medical curriculum and was admitted a licentiate of the Faculty of Physicians and Surgeons. *"It was with unfeigned delight,"* he says, *"that I became a member of a profession which is pre-eminently devoted to practical benevolence, and which with unwearied energy pursues from age to age its endeavours to lessen human woe."*

Livingstone's first project was to go to China as a medical missionary; but there being no prospect of a speedy termination to the war then waging between England and that country, he turned his thoughts to Africa, and having joined himself to the London Missionary Society, he sailed in the year 1840 for Cape Town and Algoa Bay.

Thence he proceeded inland, where he spent the following sixteen years of his life — viz., from 1840 to 1856 — in medical and missionary labours, to alleviate the heavy woes and dispel the deep spiritual darkness of the poor Africans.

In 1856 he returned to England. His fame had preceded him — accordingly a right hearty welcome was given to him by his countrymen. He soon published his *"Journal of Missionary Travels in South Africa,"* — and that book, combined with his own personal appearances on the public platform and in private life, at once stamped David Livingstone in the opinion of the whole country as one of our greatest travellers and noblest of men. And that fame of him never waned; on the contrary, it was like "the path of the just," which is *"as the morning light that shineth more and more unto the perfect day."*

How well do we remember the anxiety that was displayed when he was *lost* in the supposed *wilds* that lay beyond the confines of civilization! How eagerly was it asked again and again, wherever the English tongue was spoken — in Great Britain, America, India, Australia — *"Any news of Livingstone? Has Livingstone turned up?"* And when he did turn up — when Stanley, penetrating into the mysterious, found him worn and weary at Ujiji, and doffed his hat and greeted him in true American fashion, *"Dr Livingstone, I presume!"* — the news seemed to us too good to be true.

We threw an unjust discredit upon the young and daring traveller's story; but when, to our shame for our unbelief, the tidings were confirmed, then did a shout of gladness ascend from the whole world, and Britain, like a fond mother, yearned for the return of her noble son. But, alas! *"He cometh not,"* she said.

Our gladness was soon turned into weeping. Like a dagger to the heart the electric wire flashed the tidings — *"Livingstone is dead!"* And when the details of his death — beneath the sheltering shadow of Africa's palm-tree leaves — were made known to us, and when the echoes of his dying voice reached our country, *"I am going home, I am going home!"* then did a mourning nation send up the response — *"Yes, come home, come home; our honoured traveller shall have his long quiet rest where sleep in cherished graves many of the noblest and greatest of Britain's sons."*

By Rev Stewart Wright

"*He was one of us,*" said Dean Stanley, the day after his funeral, and standing over his grave, "*He was one of us. Like Telford or Stephenson, by whose side he now lies, he was the builder of his own fate and of his own character. What boy is there who may not be impressed by the example of that vigilant industry by which in his youthful days, amid the roar of machinery, he picked up sentence by sentence from the book which his spinning-jenny was made to support? What man is there that may not be at once stimulated and encouraged by that patient perseverance with which in his declining years, counting the obstacles of time and space for nothing, toiled through ceaseless hardships amid multiplying infirmities of body, with the sickening sense of loneliness, desertion, and disappointment, towards the attainment of the work he had set himself to do or die.*" Who is there who may not be nerved to the performance of duties, high or low, by the sight of that life-long comment of the homely maxim, treasured up by him as the family legacy of one of his rustic ancestors, "*Be honest;*" those other words addressed to him from the death-bed of a poor Scottish peasant — "*Now, lad, make religion the every-day business of your life, not a thing of fits and starts, for if you do not, temptation and other things will get the better of you.*"

Aye, Livingstone may be dead, but in the benign influences that have flowed from his life he shall live for ever, and in "*ten thousand other forms and shapes he shall walk this earth and bless it.*" The knowledge and remembrance of his noble career, stretching from the humble room in Blantyre to the honoured grave in Westminster, will so impress the minds of the young men of this country in all generations, that they will not fail to be stirred up to a righteous emulation to seek after everything that is great and good.

And, though dead, Livingstone shall yet conquer in the grand project of his life; and the evidences of this are already coming; — for the slave-holder, whom he so much hated for his cruelty, shall perish — and the *chains,* whose rattling haunted him even in his dreams, shall be broken in pieces, and the poor negro captive, for whom he prayed and yearned, shall be *free*; and the horrors of barbarism and heathenism shall give place to the influences of civilization, and the teachings of Christianity, and *a resuscitated Africa shall be the lasting monument to the greatness and goodness of David Livingstone.*

III. — THE FOUNDERS OF BLANTYRE MILLS.

"*There were giants in those days*" might truly be said, in an intellectual and commercial sense, of the merchants of Glasgow during the course of the last century. Two of the most eminent among the many were David Dale, of Rosebank, and James Monteith, of Anderston.

Of the former, Mr Stewart in his "Curiosities" justly writes — "*Of all the individuals that pass before us in our hasty survey of the old Glasgow commercial aristocracy, there are perhaps none more worthy of our respect and admiration than David Dale, who from lowly circumstances raised himself to independence and fortune; whose whole business life was most earnestly devoted to the moral and material welfare of this city, and who has left a reputation which constitutes the best memorial of his worth.*" And of the latter, Mr Stewart, with equal justice, says — "*Amongst those old Glasgow worthies, James Monteith, of Anderston, claims special attention for that robust perseverance which marked his life and associated his name with the growth and stability of the city.*"

Amongst his many great enterprises, David Dale established the spinning factory and Turkey-red dye works which have been so long known and celebrated as the "Blantyre Mills." This was in 1785. Seven years afterwards, in 1792, the mills were bought by Mr James Monteith, second son of the above-mentioned James Monteith, of Anderston, and an elder brother of the still more celebrated Henry Monteith, afterwards of Carstairs.

The story of the indefatigable energies of these two brothers in establishing their famous firm is remarkably interesting, and, with Mr Stewart's permission, we transcribe it from the "Curiosities:" — "*The year following the purchase of the mills, 1793, was a most disastrous one for Glasgow. The events which followed the French Revolution paralysed commerce everywhere, and of course fell with the greatest weight upon such manufacturing establishments as that of Blantyre, which was only in the first stage of its existence. Mr Monteith was in despair, and in fear of total ruin, waited on Mr Dale, and urged upon him to rescind their agreement; but old David was inexorable, and so there was no help for it but to make the best of a bad — a ruinous bargain — as it was considered. About this time an establishment was started in London, chiefly through the instrumentality of Provost Patrick Colquhoun, we* believe, for the sale of cotton and linen cloth by vendu — a modification of the auction mart — and it occurred to Mr Monteith that if he could get his unsaleable yarns quickly manufactured into cloth, here was a channel through which he might have them disposed of, if not with profit, at any rate with no great loss. The work was prosecuted with great energy, and so successful did the scheme turn out, that, in the course of four years, Mr Monteith, instead of finding himself a ruined manufacturer, as he had at one time anticipated, found that he had realised a fortune of £80,000. He was the chief partner in the firm of Henry Monteith & Co. He died in 1802."

"His brother Henry, born in 1764, was the best known and most highly honoured of this remarkable family. In early life he was sent to get a partial knowledge of the art of weaving, a course that was generally followed in the case of gentlemen's sons who expected to take part in the business of manufacturing. He used to boast that on the very first day that he mounted the loom he earned 'half-a-crown.' While quite a young man he established an extensive manufacturing business in Anderston. He had fallen on evil times, however. A vigorous competition at home and abroad, as well as recent improvements in the art of weaving, had made it necessary, in accordance with the ordinary laws of supply and demand, that wages should be reduced. This, of course, was received with cries of oppression and injustice. A bill was framed by the weavers for fixing the price of weaving by Act of Parliament, and loud complaints were expressed because it had been received with so little favour. The popular discontent at last found vent in open rupture, and in 1785, when Mr Monteith was only twenty-one years of age, his warehouse windows were broken, and he himself seized and roughly handled, for his "queue" was ruthlessly cut off — the loss of which would doubtless be regarded as a great degradation, being ostentatiously worn by every young man who aspired to follow the fashion.

Notwithstanding this opposition, Mr Monteith's success in life was very marked. In 1802 he established at Barrowfield a large factory for weaving Bandana handkerchiefs, which was very prosperous; and on the death of his brother James, in that same year, he took the principal management of the whole extensive business of the firm, which was then known as Henry Monteith & Co., and which, besides the Bandana factory, carried on bleaching, and subsequently extensive Turkey-red dyeing and calico printing, as well as cotton weaving and printing on a large scale. His mills at Blantyre comprised at the time, as they do still, with all the accommodation required for the comfort of the operatives — an entire town!"

Such is the story, so graphically told, of the origin of our mills. We would venture to call it both romantic and heroic, and testifying, as many such successful enterprises do, that peace has got its victories as well as war.

The mills have been a great blessing in the parish, giving to many families, generation after generation for the last hundred years, comfortable means of subsistence; and although all the works are not now in the possession of the same firm, Messrs Monteith & Co. having lately transferred the Weaving Factory to others, and retaining the Dye Works to themselves, yet the mills present the same busy scene, giving employment to hundreds.

As a general rule, working in cotton mills and dye works is not favourable to health — especially in larger towns — but there is a pleasing exception in the workers at Blantyre. Mr Miller, the late superintendent with Messrs Monteith & Co., bore the following testimony to the healthiness of the villagers in the employment of the firm forty years ago, and the same is true at the present time :— *"The people in these works are, in general, as healthy as their neighbours in other parts of the parish, many of them attaining a great age. This month one of the mechanics died aged ninety-four. There is an overseer in the service of the company seventy-seven years of age, who has been employed forty-eight years within the walls of the mill. There are several others between eighty and ninety who still enjoy good health, and not a few between seventy and eighty who are still following their usual avocations. Many workers are now employed who have been upwards of forty years in the service of the company."*

No doubt this general healthiness and longevity are owing greatly to the pure and bracing air around them; but the neatness and cleanliness of the village are likewise powerful factors towards this happy result. Messrs Monteith, who are the sole proprietors, keep scavengers and watchmen, and supply the whole village with a plentiful supply of water — both soft and hard — by means of force pumps at their works. And unceasingly, during those many years, has been the kindly interest which the members of this firm have taken to promote not only the temporal but the moral and spiritual well-being of their employees, and of those who have grown old and infirm in their service. The present head of the firm is the much esteemed Mr Hannan, the nephew of the late Mr Monteith who established the factory, his partners being his son and Mr James Reid.

The chapel, which was erected by this firm in their village about fifty years ago, and to which we have already alluded, is not now upheld, there being plenty of church accommodation in the churches that have been recently erected. Mr Reid is one of the trustees of the new and handsome Stonefield Established Church, to which his firm continue a generous support.

Nor is the long-established school in the village now open: it did a good work in its day, but the growing necessities of the parish required it to give place to the larger and more central Educational Institution in the Stonefield district.

(This chapter was written before the recent change in the firm, when Mr Hannan, sen., retired after a long and honourable career, carrying with him into the quietude of old age the affection and esteem of all; and Mr Strathern, for many years the active manager of the works, was admitted as a partner.)

Figure 5 Erskine House - The seat of Lord Blantyre

CHAPTER 4

Natural history

Not more than fifteen years ago the Lairds of Blantyre little dreamt of the rich and extensive fields of coal that lay undisturbed fathoms deep beneath the surface of the lands they inherited from their fathers. Even the wise and scientific declared unhesitatingly that of this valuable mineral there was none. Here is the record to be found in the last statistical account of the parish, strange to read it now in the light of recent discoveries, and surrounded as we are by those reeking chimneys that blacken our sky:— *"Owing to the break in the coal formation which occurs between Hamilton and Quarter, none of the principal seams of coal are wrought for many miles to the north of that particular spot. Coal has, however, been wrought on a small scale at Calderside and Rottenburn, but those are only some thin seams found beneath the seventh bed of coal, or sourmilk coal, as it is termed by the miners, all of a lean quality, and generally much interlaced with laminae of stone, blaes, and shiver."*

But this fallacy of no coal in Blantyre was speedily to be dissipated. "The proof of the pudding is the preeing of it"; so the "boring" of the soil revealed the astounding fact, which caused all the Lairds, and others too, to leap for joy, that, one hundred fathoms down, there were seams of coal of great thickness, and as excellent in quality as any to be found throughout broad Scotland. The following are the seams, the depths at which they are found, and their respective thicknesses :—

	DEPTHS	THICKNESS of COAL		
	Fathoms	Fathoms	Feet	Inches
To Upper Coal	104		2	6
From Upper Coal to Ell Coal	16		4	9
From Ell Coal to	9		4	0

Pyotshaw Coal			
From Pyotshaw Coal to Main Coal	2	4	3
From Main Coal to Humph Coal	10	2	9
From Humph Coal to Splint Coal	4	4	0
From Splint Coal to Virgin Coal	0	2	9

These large coal-fields are being busily wrought by the Messrs Dixon (Limited), Messrs Merry and Cunningham, and the Messrs Baird. The first mentioned firm brings to the surface about 1,200 tons daily, and the second about half that quantity. The Messrs Baird produce a smaller amount, as they have more recently commenced operations, and the fields they have in this parish are not so large as those held by either of the other two. Miners are constantly at work.

It was this "big find," as our Yankee cousins would say, which at once revolutionized our parish. The *"quiet and rural retreat,"* — *"Sweet Auburn, loveliest village of the plain"* — disappeared; and in its place arose the grim and noisy centre of Industry and Trade, with its interminable rows of colliers' red-bricked cottages. The old folks shake their heads, and mournfully say, *"The parish is no' what it was,"* clearly implying thereby that the *"old was best"* whilst the new-comers boast that they have roused us out of our *"sleepy-hollow,"* and brought riches and plenty to our very doors. It is the old story of *"the shield,"* — pure gold to one, dirty brass to another, just according to the point from which it was viewed.

Our parish likewise abounds with ironstone, especially the upper or southern ranges of it, which for a hundred years or more has been wrought by Messrs Colin Dunlop and Co. *"At Blackcraig, near Calderwood, seventeen seams of ironstone may be counted, the one above the other; a sight, it is believed, not to be met with anywhere else in the world."* The same firm have also wrought the limestone, which is found at Auchintibber.

By Rev Stewart Wright

That which underlies the surface at Calderside is wrought by the proprietor, Mr Anderson, by whom it is manufactured into very fine Roman cement.

The last statistical account has the following remarks upon this section of rocks, which is called the upper or anvil band of limestone, and which is fourteen inches thick :— *"It draws its name from the lime-rock being dislocated throughout, and apparently weatherworn, so as to form blocks resembling a blacksmith's anvil, and some of them are not unlike the skeleton of a horse's head. Below this band there is a stratum of ten feet of blaes; this is succeeded by the middle seam of limestone two feet thick, beneath which is three feet of blaes overlaying the under bed of limestone, which is four feet thick. There are a great many petrifactions in the blaes, of which hundreds may be picked up. In the waste beside the mines where the blaes lies mouldering away under the influence of the sun and air, they occur in myriads, and are carried away in great numbers by the curious."*

It is interesting to note that amongst those *"curious,"* or, as we should call them, *"amateur geologists,"* of sixty years ago, was a boy whom we are all proud to remember was a native of our parish. Here is what David Livingstone tells us, in his autobiography, of some of his boyhood's pleasures :— *"Limited as my time was, I found opportunity to scour the whole countryside 'collecting samples.' These excursions, often in company with brothers, one now in Canada, and the other a clergyman in the United States, gratified my intense love of nature; and though we generally returned so unmercifully hungry and fatigued that the embryo parson shed tears, yet we discovered so many, to us, new and interesting things, that he was always as eager to join us next time as he was the last. On one of those exploring tours we entered a limestone quarry — long before geology was as popular as it is now. It is impossible to describe the delight and wonder with which I began to collect the shells found in the carboniferous limestone which crops out in High Blantyre and Cambuslang.*

A quarryman, seeing a little boy so engaged, looked with that pitying eye which the benevolent assume when viewing the insane. He addressed him with "However did these shells come into these rocks?" "When God made the rocks, he made the shells in them," was the damping reply. What a deal of trouble geologists might have saved themselves by adopting the Turk-like philosophy of this Scotchman?"

The following is a valuable contribution on the "*Geology of Blantyre,*" which has been kindly sent to us by our predecessor, Dr Gloag :—

1. Red sandstones, probably belonging to the Permean formation.
2. The upper coal-measures.
3. The carboniferous limestone, including (a), cement stone and limestone of Calderside, and (b), Crossbasket ironstone and limestone.

"In the Parish there are two or three localities where fossils are found. At Calderside, in the limestone several remarkable fossils have been found, especially some of the largest cephalopoda, as the Nautilus and Actinoceras, and a remarkable nut, first found in the cement limestones at Calderside, and subsequently in the same strata at East Kilbride, which has received the name Trigonocarpum. Up the Sides road, about a mile and half from High Blantyre, on the left side, are the Newfield quarries, which have been thoroughly searched by members of the Geological Society of Glasgow, and which have yielded a great variety of species. On the right side of the road there is Broomhouse quarry, which is a continuation of the Newfield section. When first I came to Blantyre in 1841, the shells lying in this quarry were as numerous as those on the sea shore. The most numerous among them were the Leda attenuata and the Nucula gibbosa, specimens of both of which were found in very finest condition. Since then, however, the quarry has been repeatedly searched by amateur geologists, and the fossils have become rare.

The following is a list of the fossils found in the limestones of the district, an asterisk, being affixed to those which were found by myself :—

a	Plantae		Adiantes Lindsaeformis
			Trigoncarpam Gloagianum
b	Protozoa Foraminifera	:	Endothyra Bowmanni
			Endothyra globolus
			Stacheia fusiformis

		Trochammina incerta	
		Valvulina plicata	
c	Actinozoa	Stenopora tumida	*
d	Echinodermata	Hydreionocrinus Scoticus	*
		Pisocrinus globularis	
		Poteriocrinus crassus	*
		Numerous fingers and stems of crinoids of generaactinocrinus and platycrinus	*
e	Annelida	Ortonia carbonaria	
		Serpulites membranacius	*
f	Crustacea	Bairdia plebeia	
		Bairdia subcylindrica	
		Beyrichia bituberculata	
		Cythere cuneola	
		Griffithides mesotuberculatus	*
		Kirkbya Urei	
g	Polyzoa	Actinostoma fenestratum	*
		Archaeopora nexilis	*
		Ceriopora interporosa	
		Cerampora(Diastopora) megastoma	*
		Fenestella plebeia	*
		Fenestella tuberculo-carinata	*

		Glauconome elegans	
		Glauconome flexicarinata	
		Glauconome marginalis	
		Glauconome stellipora	
		Hyphasmopora Buskii	
		Rhabdomeson gracile	
		Synocladia carbonaria	
		Synocladia fenestelliformis	
h	Brachiopoda	Athyris ambigua	*
		Chonetes Laguessiana	*
		Crania quadrata	*
		Discina nitida	*
h	Brachiopoda continued	Lingula mytiloides	*
		Productus longispinus	*
		Productus giganteus	
		Productus semireticulatus	
		Productus var. Martini	*
		Productus Toungianus	
		Rhynchonella pleurodon	*
		Spirifera bisulcata	
		Spirifera trigonalis	
		Spiriferina octoplicata	*

		Terebratula hastata	*
i	Lamellibranchiata monomyaria		
		Aviculopecten arenosus	*
		Aviculopecten fimbriatus	
		Aviculopecten ornatus	
		Pecten Sowerbii	*
j	Lamellibranchiata dimyaria	Axinus axiniformis	*
		Cardiomorpha orbicularis	
		Edmondia Egertoni	
		Edmondia rudis	*
		Edmondia unioniformis	*
		Leda attenuata	*
		Leptodomus costellatus (Boghead)	*
		Myacites sulcata	*
		Nucula gibbosa	*
		Nucula unilateralis	
		Sanguinolites tricostatus	
		Sanguinolites vaiabilis	*
k	Gasteropoda	Euomphalus Dionysii	
		Machrocheilus Michotianus	*
		Murchisonia Urei	

		Naticopsis elongata	
		Platyceras neritoides	
		Pleurotomaria contraria	
		Pleurotomaria monilifera	
l	Heteropoda	Bellerophon striatus	
		Bellerophon Urei	
m	Pteropoda	Conularia quadrisulcata	*
n	Cephalopoda	Actinoceras giganteum	*
		Goniatites striatus	
		Nautilus ingens	*
		Nautilus Leveilleanus	
		Nautilus sulcatus	
		Orthoceras attenuatum	*
		Orthoceras Breynii	
		Orthoceras undatum	*
		Poterioceras ventricosum	
o	Pisces	Leptacanthus Jenkinsoni	
		Megalichthys Hibberti	
o	Pisces	Petalodus Hastingsiae	*
		Psammodus porosus	
		Rhizodus Hibberti	
		Tomodus convexus	

By Rev Stewart Wright

The Flora of Blantyre is not materially different from the other parishes in the Middle Ward of Lanarkshire. In the moors in the upper part of the parish several good upland plants are found, but the most interesting ground for the botanist is the Calderwood Glen and the woods on the Banks of the Clyde round Blantyre Priory. In the latter, among others that we have known, the following are found in more or less abundance:— Adoxa, Moschatellina, Stellaria, Nemorum, Geranium, Phalum, Ribes Alpinum, Chrysosplenium, Alternifolium, Campanala Latifolia, Veronica Montana, and Melica Uniflora. There is a considerable variety of ferns in the parish. Among others, the Oak, Beech, Shield, Buckler, Sweetscented, Hart's Tongue, Brittle, Black Spleenwort, Maidenhair Spleenwort, Wall Rue, Hard, Male, and Lady Ferns, are all found in various localities.

There are various mineral springs throughout the parish, especially on the banks of the Calder, where the iron and lime abound: but the spring *par excellence* is that which is in a field in the farm of Blantyre Park. The history of this well, which some people facetiously call the "*Blantyre Spa*," was lately given by us in a communication to the *Glasgow Herald,* and which we here transcribe. It was headed —

A Curious Phenomenon.

There is a district in this parish which is known as "Auchintibber," a name derived from two Gaelic words which signify "*The field of the healing waters.*" The evident reason why it was so called was from the existence of a mineral spring, which was in much repute and greatly resorted to in former days.

In a statistical account of the parish, written a hundred years ago by the Minister, he says that the water of this well was very frequently and successfully used for sore eyes, scorbutic diseases, and many other complaints. The smell of it was sulphurous, and the taste of it as rotten eggs. And there is stated, as evidence of its healing properties, that there was in the hands of "*The Heritors, Ministers, and Kirk-session,*" a sum of money, amounting to £213 13s., which comprised "*The donations left to the poor of the parish by benevolent persons who occasionally resorted to this part of the country to enjoy the benefits of the well at Park.*" Unfortunately, about half a century ago, this well dried up, its waters ceased to rise when the iron-stone pits were sunk; and such it has remained, until within the last fortnight, when, strange to say, in an instant it sprang again into active existence, and its waters are now flowing up in great abundance, having the same strong sulphurous smell, the same abominable taste of rotten eggs, but, no doubt, the same *"healing powers."* I should say that the properties of the water are very similar to those of the famed well at Moffat.

Since writing the above, we find that the waters of this Blantyre well and those of St Bernard's Well in Edinburgh are exactly the same in their component parts. The following is the results of an analysis which was made a short time ago by Mr Thomson, Chemist, at the Govan Iron Works:—

Grains per Gallon.

	Carbonate of Lime	23.20	
	Sulphate of Lime	2.42	
"The solid is The also	Carbonate of Magnesia	16.00	total matter 62.00. water
	Sulphate of Magnesia	12.82	
	Carbonate of Soda	1.72	
	total	56.16	

contains some sulphurated hydrogen gas dissolved through it."

CHAPTER 5

Miscellaneous

POPULATION

Exactly one hundred years ago our predecessor, Mr Stevenson, tells us that the number of families in the parish was 130, and the total number of inhabitants was 520, and that this had been about the extent of the population *"as far as can be traced back."* But very soon after this period, in 1785, the population received a great and immediate increase by the opening of the Blantyre Cotton Mills on the banks of the Clyde by Messrs. Henry Monteith & Co.; it bounded up at once to 1751, and continued to make steady progress until 1831, when it reached a total of 3000. At this figure, or little over it, the population remained for 40 years, making no advancement until after 1871, when our great coal fields were discovered and began to be wrought. And so, the last decade has seen the wonderful increase of population from about 3,000 to over 10,000.

Here is another contrast. The annual number of births within the parish for ten years preceding 1783 was 17, of deaths during the same period 11, and of marriages 6; whereas during the last ten years the annual number of births has been 440, of deaths 180, and of marriages 78. What an easy time of it our predecessors must have had! No wonder that one of them wrote such tremendous long sermons; and that another, to employ his leisure hours, rented some fields beside his glebe, and was famed for his cultivation of turnips and cabbages! Why, on one Sunday afternoon, more than once, after Divine services, we have baptised more children than were born in a year throughout the whole parish less than a century ago.

EDUCATION

The parish schools likewise mark progress in a wonderful manner. What does Mr Stevenson tell us under this head? *"There is only one school in the parish. The schoolmaster's salary is about £6, but he has neither house nor garden belonging to the office. The number of* scholars is usually about 50; and the whole living may amount to about £20 per annum." Ponder upon this and be grateful ye who, in those modern times, are appointed "*To teach the young idea how to shoot.*"

And what a school-room it was, where our forefathers were taught and pawmied! None of your palatial edifices as we have now, but a low thatched-roofed hut, standing at one corner of the graveyard, where the snow and the rain found an easy ingress, even to the very "hearthstone," and the cold wind, "blawing loud wi' angry sugh," was kept out by urchins as best they could, for they stuffed an old hat of the "maisters," and a bonnet of one of the boys into the broken panes. Let us be exact about this ancient educational institution. At a general meeting of the Heritors of Blantyre, held on the 18th of May, 1731, the following minute was unanimously passed :— "*The Heritors taking to their consideration that notwithstanding by the 9th Act of the session of the fifth Parliament of King William, it is expressly stated and ordained that the Heritors of each parish meet and provide a commodious house for a school, yet they have never had any such school, and in order to supply that defect they have agreed to build a house 22 feet long and 18 feet wide on the south side corner of the Church-yard, at a cost of one hundred pounds Scots.*"

That is the picture of the past; let us turn from it to contemplate the present, for here are our Parish Schools as they are in this year of grace 1883. We quote from a notice written by ourselves in our local magazine a few months ago :—

"*At the monthly meeting of our School Board, there was submitted the usual 'attendance' of pupils. How large the number! and how forcibly it tells of the great and rapid increase of population which has characterised our parish in recent years. In our two Public Schools there were enrolled, in the month of February, 1223 pupils, and the average attendance was 996; whilst the two Roman Catholic Schools had on their rolls 540, the average attendance being 388. The prevalence of hooping cough in the Stonefield district has prevented many children from being regularly present.*

"*In the year 1875 — just about eight years ago — when our two Schools were opened, the then Chairman of the Board (who happened to be the Parish Minister) in his opening address, ventured to predict that those edifices, large and commodious as they were — some people thinking them too large — were scarcely able to meet the requirements of the parish, and that not many years would elapse ere another school or schools of equal size and dimensions would need to be built. This prediction has been verified. Since that time, two large additions have been made to those schools, capable of containing nearly 300 pupils; whilst the Roman Catholic community have built schools for themselves. Thus do those crowded edifices tell of the wonderful growth of our population.*

From a short statistical account of the parish now before us, we find that not more than twenty years ago there were only 50 scholars attending the Parochial School in High Blantyre village, and about 100 in the excellent school that was established and supported for so many years by Messrs. Henry Monteith & Co. for the benefit of the children of their workers. Well, it is to be confidently expected that those superior educational institutions of our day, which have been erected at so much expense to the parishioners, will do as good, if not much better, work in their day than has been done by the parochial and private schools of olden times. These served the country well for centuries.

Out of their lowly doors have gone forth some of the most eminent of men — none more justly honoured than David Livingstone, born and bred in Blantyre. And Scotchmen there have been, and still are, who have gratefully and joyfully acknowledged that the prominent positions they have been enabled to take amongst their fellowmen, both in their own country and in other lands, have been greatly due to the thorough education they received in our old Parish Schools. These are now gone, but we can testify to their worth. May our children unto many generations be able to bear even a better testimony to the great value of our imposing national schools. Their present efficiency is certainly a good guarantee for the future. The recent reports by the Government Inspectors are most satisfactory, and very creditable to both teachers and taught. At his last report, one of those officials made the following entry in the log book of Low Blantyre School :— 'I visited the school this day (13th February), and found everything in excellent order. The new class-rooms are now ready for occupation, and form a handsome addition to the school buildings. Their spaciousness and the admirable way in which they have been furnished reflect the utmost credit on the enlightened liberality of the Board.'"

PAROCHIAL STATISTICS

Our readers, especially those who are resident in the parish, and have painful experience of taxes, will scarcely credit the fact that less than a hundred years ago there were in this then Arcadian Blantyre only four or five paupers on the parish roll, and that the *"heritors and kirk-session had a stock for the support of the poor amounting to about £200; the interest of which, together with the weekly collections, afforded a comfortable supply for the indigent."* We have been indulging in contrasts illustrative of our progress in many respects, but here we must hide our diminished heads, and acknowledge that as to pauperism and indigence, the advantage lay decidedly with *"the good old times."* Think of it; a century ago there were but five paupers within the bounds of a parish that has now on its roll —

Of Registered Poor and Dependents,	128
— Casual Poor and Dependents,	46
— Registered Poor and Dependents paid for other parishes,	122
Total,	296

This is not a pleasant contrast, and forces us to question, after all, the genuineness of our boasted progress. True, indeed, we have advanced greatly in power and wealth, in scientific knowledge, sanitary improvements, and otherwise; but has there not been a corresponding advancement in thriftlessness, criminality, and pauperism. The higher the heights we have attained the longer and deeper the shadows that fall over the plain. The valued rental of the parish in 1783 was £1,684 11s. 8d. Scots; the present total valuation is £40,338 sterling. This comprises —

Valuation of Heritors' Lands,	£5,312	6 0
" " Houses and Workhops,	£17,582	18 0
" " Minerals,	£13,191	16 0
" " Railways,	£4,251	0 0

By Rev Stewart Wright

ANCIENT RELICS

From time to time urns have been dug up in various fields throughout the parish. Mr Stevenson mentions that in his day *"some were found in a large heap of stones. In the centre of the heap, square stones were placed so as to form a kind of chest, and the urns were placed within it. They contained a kind of unctuous earthy substance; and some remains of bones were scattered around them."* These were given to the College of Glasgow, where no doubt they still are. Then again, about forty years ago, a stone coffin, with an urn standing in one corner of it, was turned up at Shott, near the parish church. A skull, almost entire, was found in it, and nearly the whole of the teeth were in good preservation. The urn was of baked earth, seemingly only sun-dried, five and a half inches high, and the same across the mouth. Fragments of larger urns, better burned and more highly ornamented, were found in other parts of the field. And at a later period, in this same field; which is called the Archers' Croft, on its being turned up to form the embankments of the railway, were discovered various stone coffins. And a woman who lives in a cottage close by the field, has in her possession an urn which her father dug up when delving in his garden.

These sepulchral urns give undoubted evidence that in a far back time, long before the Romano-British period, this Archer's field was a burying place of the dead. A celebrated archaeologist makes the following remarks with reference to them :— *"The use of the sepulchral urn must be regarded as in itself a proof of some degree of progress. The earliest of these, however, are of the rudest possible description. They are fashioned with the hand, of coarse clay, by workmen ignorant of the turning lathe or wheel of the potter. They are generally unsymmetrical, merely dried in the sun, without any attempt at design, and devoid of ornament. Of a later period, though still accompanied only with weapons and implements of stone, the urn is found neatly fashioned into various forms, and ornamented with different patterns of lines, traced by some instrument in the soft clay, after which the vessel has been baked with fire. The great number of these urns which have been found, and the abundance of stone and flint weapons scattered over the whole British Islands, and, indeed, over most parts of Europe, furnish evidence of the same rude tribes having continued with little change to occupy Europe during many generations. A change, however, of a most decided character broke in at length on the barbarous habits of this primitive British race, not improbably by the irruption of more civilised tribes from the East."*

There is another relic of antiquity to be found further up in the parish. "It is a singular conical hill at Calderside, which goes by the name of the Camp-Knowe. It is 600 feet in circumference, and was anciently surrounded by a ditch. Near the same spot a subterranean structure made of flags, like the sole of an oven, was lately discovered. We should be pleased to hear of excavations made into the Camp-Knowe. It is undoubtedly of great antiquity, constructed by the earliest inhabitants of the Island as a sort of fortress for their safety, and the protection of their goods when threatened by invading foes. The archaeologist from whom we have already quoted, makes the following observations regarding these earthen Duns or Mounds :— *"The summits of numerous hills in Scotland, Ireland, and Wales, retain traces of ancient hill-forts of various descriptions, from the earthen ramparts of the circular down to the elaborately constructed borgh or stone fort which is still to be found, chiefly in the Orkneys and Western Isles. Some of the simplest earthen duns, consisting of a round or oval earthen wall and ditch surmounting a rising ground, may be presumed to be the work of the same rude architects who occupied the pit dwellings and constructed the earthen cattle folds already described."*

We must not here omit to mention that the field, close by the manse, where have been found the urns and stone coffins, is said to have got its name of *"Archers' Croft"* from being the field where the young villagers, in the time of Bruce and Wallace and the first Stuarts, were wont to meet for the practice of archery: *"it being the great pastime of the lower classes, which they were bound by Royal Proclamation to practise on Sundays and holidays after Divine service."* The Archers' Croft was the rifle range of olden times.

THE STORY OF THE EXPLOSION

The annals of our parish would certainly not be complete without some allusion to that catastrophe which so recently brought it out of its obscurity into a sad prominence before the whole world, we mean the Pit Explosion which took place on the morning of the 22nd October, 1877. Up till then Scotland had been peculiarly fortunate in being exempted from those terrible colliery accidents which were too often experienced by the mining communities of England and Wales. But now its turn had come; and a record was to be made in a page of its history, of one of the most devastating explosions as had happened in any land. By it, in a moment, in the twinkling of an eye," 218, if not more, men and boys were killed, leaving behind them, to the mercy of God and man, 106 widows, 300 fatherless children, and about 50 other relatives, such as aged parents, who were more or less dependent upon the dead.

What a gloomy morning that October Monday was. How indelibly is it engraven on our memory. We were dressing at the time. The window of our room looked over against the pits. A sudden flash darted up from the most distant shaft, accompanied by debris, and a report not very loud; then forthwith there arose from the shaft nearest to us a dense volume of smoke, "the blackness of darkness," which spread itself, a terrible funeral pall, over the surrounding plain. We were soon at the scene of the disaster, whither hundreds of eager and terrified creatures were hurrying, and there for hours we remained, a stricken shepherd amongst a stricken flock. The one shaft was blocked up with ruins, but the other was partially clear; again and again did gallant men descend to rescue, if possible, their buried comrades but all in vain; they merely succeeded in bringing up a few dead bodies, when they themselves were overpowered by the choke damp and had to be brought up to the surface. Some of them were more dead than alive, and it was with difficulty we succeeded in restoring them.

Still, no matter the danger, there were no lack of volunteers, many of them wildly demanding to be lowered down, until at last, when the short winter's day was drawing to a close, imperative orders were issued that no more lives were to be risked. Then hope fled; and the agonised crowd were left in the darkness and pityless rain to face the terribleness in its magnitude that not one of the two hundred miners and more, that were entombed beneath us, would ever see the light. Nor did they. Day after day, for three weeks following, and after laborious exertions, were the bodies found and brought up for interment. With the exception of the Roman Catholics, and there were not many of them, and a few others, all the dead were laid side by side in two long trenches that had been dug in the newly made cemetery. The report of the funerals in one evening, as given in the *Herald,* was characteristic of them all :— *"The scene in the Parish Burying-ground, where the bodies were interred, was very impressive, and by the time that Mr. Wright got as far in the service as 'Earth to earth, ashes to ashes, dust to dust,' many of the onlookers were in tears. Few of them will soon forget the sight — the cold grey twilight, the dark overcast sky, the long deep trench, the silent uncovered multitude, and the solemn tones of the preacher's voice."*

A handsome granite monument, in the shape of an obelisk, is now erected over the graves of the poor miners. It has the following inscription : —

> *"Erected by WILLIAM DIXON, Limited, in*
> *Memory of 240 of their Workmen who were*
> *Killed by Explosions in Blantyre Colliery,*
> *on 22nd October, 1877, and 2nd July, 1879;*
> *and many of whom are buried here."*

Gradually the dead were buried; but the living remained, bereft of their bread winners. No time was to be lost; starvation must be averted; so on the morning after the disaster, surrounded by widows and orphans, we issued, through the kindly reporters, the following appeal: — *"We, the undersigned, appeal to the sympathies of the nation in behalf of the mothers, wives, and orphans, who have, in very many cases, been rendered perfectly destitute by the terrible colliery explosion which has occurred in this district. 218 men and boys have been killed, all the male members of several families have been swept away, and widespread desolation prevails. There is 'lamentation and bitter weeping.' Contributions are earnestly solicited to meet the destitution of the afflicted families."* And what a response came to that appeal! The rich man's thousand and the widow's mite; the noble lady's gift of a hundred mourning dresses, and the orphan girl's gift of a few pairs of warm, knitted stockings. Here is still before us the pile of letters which we keep with a kind of reverential feeling, for they tell of the noble sympathy and brotherly kindness of a whole nation, from our beloved Queen to some of the poorest in her realm.

The citizens of Glasgow were not slow to take up the cause of the bereaved. A meeting was called together by the Lord Provost, when an influential committee was appointed to collect subscriptions, and frame rules for the distribution of relief. Through their exertions, the contributions speedily reached the magnificent total of £48,246; and under their unwearied superintendence the remaining widows and orphans still receive their allowances. They have never known a moment's want, and never will, as long as they continue on this fund. What a blessing it has been; and how earnestly we wish that such a fund was in existence on the wide basis, to meet the destitution arising from accidents, serious and fatal, that are continually happening in our mining districts.

Before closing this short record of the "Explosion," we must not fail to pay a just tribute of praise to the gallant conduct of the miners, as we ourselves witnessed on that calamitous day, and for many days afterwards. Better than any words of ours could do, were they thus spoken of by the reporter of the *Daily Telegraph*: — *"The British miner can fight with as much 'strength and majesty' as the British soldier. If one fall in the imminent deadly breach, another coolly takes his place, and carries on the assault with a sublime unconsciousness of any odds that may be against him. So it was at High Blantyre. When a disabled hero was brought to bank and carefully covered with earth to free him from the influence of the poisonous gas, ten more were eager to descend into the depths and risk a similar fate, or worse. We are glad to think that there are thousands upon thousands of men in these islands who know that they themselves would have done the same had they been present. Yet few are able to realise the circumstances amid which the noble Scotchmen proved their bravery and devotion. A battlefield is ghastly enough, and its horrors might well appal those who look upon them. The soldier, however, has all the excitement of personal conflict, and sometimes a burning thirst for revenge, to sustain him; whereas, in the High Blantyre mine, the rescuers struggled against an invisible foe, whose distinctiveness was evidenced on every side in the most horrible forms.*

The other day we paid a tribute of admiration to Welshmen; now it is Scotchmen who claim a like reward. In due time, when the two hundred bodies shall have been brought up, and consigned by loving hands to their last resting place, the cause of the disaster will receive attention, a jury will return a verdict, and a Government inspector will make his report. But all this has been done often before, and we seem as far off as ever from the ability to protect our miners against the dangers that surround their calling."

VOLUNTEER MOVEMENT

The Parish of Blantyre was not behind, when in the year 1859 there was a general movement all over England and Scotland to raise regiments of citizen soldiers for the defence of their country, and towards the close of the above year a meeting was held in the Free Church to take steps for the formation of a company comprised of inhabitants of the parish.

The success of the project was so great that early in the year 1860 a company of Volunteers, of nearly one hundred men, had commenced drilling in a large hall in the works of Henry Monteith & Co., at Low Blantyre, their services accepted by Government, and officers appointed and duly gazetted. The first officers of the Blantyre Volunteer Company (now D Company of the 2nd Lanarkshire Rifle Volunteers) were Captain James Reid (afterwards Lieut.-Colonel of the Regiment); Lieut. James Hutton Watkins (now deceased), and Ensign Robert Valentine Reid (now in India).

The company was sworn-in by the late Sheriff Veitch of Hamilton at a social meeting held in the spring of the year 1860 in the School-room of Low Blantyre village, and in August of the same year, to the number of upwards of one hundred, was present at the great Volunteer Review, held by Her Majesty in Edinburgh, when more than twenty-two thousand Scottish Volunteers assembled in the Queen's Park in that city.

The Government of that day (1859-1860) were not very liberal to the Volunteers, so that the cost of equipment had to be met to some extent by subscriptions raised from friends in the parish, and as some of the principal proprietors considered this movement to be of rather an evanescent character, declined to give any assistance. However, it is proper to state that the firm of Henry Monteith & Co., Robert Ker, Esq., of Auchenraith; the late James Clark, Esq., of Crossbasket, and a few others, came forward with very liberal sums, which more than paid the cost of raising the company and putting it on a sound financial footing. It is unnecessary here to say anything about the doubts then expressed as to the lasting nature of the Volunteer movement which was so largely shared by so many proprietors in Blantyre, for the past twenty-three years' history of Volunteering entirely disproves any such theory, and the large Volunteer army in the country has become an acknowledged institution as well as an important factor in reducing part of the national taxes which otherwise would be much greater for the support of a much larger army and navy.

ANECDOTES

The following is an old ballad by Monk Lewis. As it embodies a local legend, we insert it here, being a curiosity, although it tells against our ancient "Priorie" :—

BOTHWELL'S BONNY JANE

Loud roars the north round Bothwell's hall,
And fast descends the pattering rain,
But streams of tears still faster fall
From thy blue eyes, Oh! bonny Jane!

Hark! hark! I hear with mournful yell,
The wraiths of angry Clyde complain,
But sorrow bursts with louder swell
From thy blue eyes, Oh! bonny Jane!

Tap! tap! Who knocks? The door unfolds,
The mourner lifts her melting eyes,
And soon with joy and hope beholds
A reverend monk approaching nigh.

His air is mild, his step is slow,
His hands across his breast are laid,
And soft he sighs, while bending low,
"St. Bothan guard thee, gentle maid."

To meet the friar the damsel ran,
She kissed his hand, she clasp'd his knee,
"Now free me, free me, holy man,
Who com'st from Blantyre Priorie."

What mean those piteous cries, daughter?
St. Bothan be thy speed!
Why swim in tears thine eyes, daughter?
From whom would'st thou be freed?"

"Oh ! Father, father ! Know, my sire,
Though I long knelt, and wept, and sigh'd,
Hath sworn, ere twice ten days expire,
His Jane shall be Lord Malcolm's bride."

"Lord Malcolm is rich and great, daughter,
And comes of an high degree,
He's fit to be thy mate, daughter,
So Benedicité."

"Oh Father, father; say not so !
Though rich his halls, tho' fair his bowers,
There stands a hut where Tweed doth flow
I prize beyond Lord Malcolm's towers:

There dwells a youth where Tweed doth glide,
On whom no rank nor fortune smiles,
I'd rather be that peasant's bride
Than reign o'er all Lord Malcolm's isles."

"But should you flee away, daughter,
And wed with a village clown,
What would your father say, daughter ?
How he would fume and frown ?"

"Oh ! he might frown and he might fume,
And Malcolm's heart might grieve and pine,
So Edgar's hut for me had room,
And Edgar's lips were pressed to mine !"

"If at the Castle gate, daughter,
At night thy love so true
Should with a courser wait, daughter —
What, daughter, would'st thou do ?"

"With noiseless step the stairs I'd press,
Enclose the gate, and mount with glee,
And, ever as on I sped, would bless
The Abbot of Blantyre Priorie !"

"Then, daughter, dry those eyes so bright,
I'll haste where flows Tweed's silver stream ;

By Rev Stewart Wright

And when thou see'st, at dead of night,
A lamp in Blantyre's chapel gleam,

With noiseless step the staircase press,
For know thy lover there will be,
Then mount his steed, haste on, and bless
The Abbot of Blantyre Priorie !"

Then forth the Abbot bent his way,
While lightly danced the maiden's heart,
Oh ! how she chid the length of day,
And sighed to see the sun depart !

How joy'd she when eve's shadows came,
How swiftly gained her towers so high, —
Does there in Blantyre shine a flame ?
Ah no ! The moon deceived mine eye !"

Again the shades of evening lour ;
Again she hails the approach of night, —
Shines there a flame in Blantyre tower ?
Ah no ! — 'Tis but a northern light !

But when arrived All-Hallowe'en,
What time the night and morn divide ;
The signal lamp by Jane, was seen
To glimmer on the waves of Clyde.

She cares not for her father's tears,
She feels not for her father's sighs ;
No voice but headlong love's she hears,
And down the staircase swift she hies.

Though thrice the brownie shriek'd "Beware,"
Though thrice was heard a dying groan,
She oped the castle gate — Lo ! there
She found the friendly monk alone.

"Oh ! where is Edgar, father, say ?"
"On ! on !" the friendly monk replied.
"He fear'd his berry-brown steed would neigh,
And waits us on the banks of Clyde."

Then on they hurried, and on they hied,
Down Bothwell's slopes so steep and green,
And soon they reached the river's side,
Alas! no Edgar could be seen.

Then, Bonny Jane, thy spirits sank ;
Filled was thy heart with strange alarms :
"Now, thou art mine !" exclaimed the monk,
And clasp'd her in his ruffian arms.

"Know, yonder bark must bear thee straight
Where Blantyre owns my gay controul ;
There love and joy to greet thee wait,
There pleasure crowns for thee her bowl,"

"Long have lov'd thee, Bonny Jane,
Long breath'd to thee my secret vow ;
Come then, sweet maid ! Nay, strife is vain,
Not heaven itself can save thee now !"

The damsel shriek'd, and would have fled,
When lo ! his poniard pressed her throat !
"One cry, and 'tis your last !" he said,
And bore her fainting to the boat.

The moon shone bright, the winds were chain'd,
The boatman swiftly plied his oar ;
But, ere the river's midst was gain'd,
The tempest fiend was heard to roar.

Rain fell in sheets ; high swell'd the Clyde ;
Blue flamed the lightning's blasting brand ;
"Oh ! lighten the bark !" the boatman cries,
"Or hope no more to reach the strand.

"E'en now we stand on danger's brink,
E'en now the boat half-filled I see !
Oh ! lighten it quick, or else we sink,
Oh ! lighten it of your gay ladie."

With shrieks the maid his counsel hears ;
But vain are now her prayers, her cries,

By Rev Stewart Wright

Who car'd not for her father's tears,
Who felt not for her father's sighs !

Fear conquered love ! in wild despair
The Abbot viewed the watery grave,
Then seized the victim's golden hair,
And plunged her in the foaming wave !

She screams ! she sinks ! "Row, boatman, row !
The bark is light !" the Abbot cries ;
"Row, boatman, row to land !" When lo !
Gigantic grew the boatman's size !

With burning steel his temples bound
Throbb'd quick and high, with fiery pangs ;
He roll'd his blood-shot eyeballs round,
And furious gnashed his iron fangs ;

His hands two gore-fed scorpions grasp'd,
His eyes full joy and sight express'd.
"Thy cup is full !" he said, and clasp'd
The Abbot to his burning breast.

With hideous yell down sinks the boat,
And straight the warring winds subside,
Moon-silvered clouds through ether floats,
And gently murmuring flows the Clyde.

Since then full many a winter's powers,
In chains of ice, the earth hath bound,
And many a spring with blushing flowers,
And herbage gay, has robed the ground.

Yet legend says, at Hallowe'en,
When silence holds her deepest reign,
That still the ferryman fiend is seen
To waft the monk and bonny Jane.

And still does Blantyre's wreck display
The signal-lamp at midnight hour ;
And still to watch its fatal ray
The phantom fair haunts Bothwell Tower ;

Still tunes her lute to Edgar's name ;
Still chides the hours which stay her flight ;
Still sings, "In Blantyre shines a flame ?
Ah ! no ! 'Tis but the northern light !"

Figure 6 Bridge at Milheugh

Here is a pretty story of the "*Covenanting times*" :—

Maxwell of Shott was an officer in Claverhouse's regiment of dragoons. He was roused out of his bed one night by the clattering of horse's hoofs, and the loud shout of his captain, *"Come along, Maxwell, we have at last ferreted out the fox."* He was alluding to John Brown, the Christian carrier of Priesthill. Maxwell, in obedience to orders, was soon in the stable, saddling his steed, but his young wife followed him, and besought him earnestly that he would not go abroad on such a cruel and unrighteous expedition. Seeing all her entreaties availed nothing, she cast herself on the pavement at the stable door, and said to her husband, *"Well, if you will go, it must be over my dead and mangled body, for I too will suffer with this persecuted people."* But the noble horse stepped gently over the prostrate lady, and Maxwell rode quickly after his leader to perpetrate a deed as cold-blooded and barbarously savage as any that stains the pages of history.

By Rev Stewart Wright

This is the story as told by Sir Walter Scott.

We give it for the benefit of our young readers, that they may remember the undaunted fortitude of both men and women, in those times of persecution, when holding by what they believed to be the cause of God :—

"There lived at this gloomy period, at a place called Presthill, or Priesthill, in Lanarkshire, a man named John Brown, a Carrier by profession, and called, from his zealous religious principles, the Christian Carrier. This person had been out with the insurgents at Bothwell bridge, and was for other reasons amenable to the cruelty of the existing laws. On a morning of May, 1685, Peden, one of the Cameronian ministers, whom Brown had sheltered in his house, took his leave of his host and his wife, repeating twice, *'Poor woman! a fearful morning — a dark and misty morning!'* words which were afterwards believed to be prophetic of calamity. When Peden was gone, Brown left his house with a spade in his hand for his ordinary labour, when he was suddenly surrounded and arrested by a band of horse, with Claverhouse at their head. Although the prisoner had a hesitation in his speech on ordinary occasions, he answered the questions which were put to him in this extremity with such composure and firmness, that Claverhouse asked whether he was a preacher. He was answered in the negative. *'If he has not preached,'* said Claverhouse, *'mickle hath he prayed in his time. — But betake you now to your prayers for the last time'* (addressing the sufferer), *'for you shall presently die.'*

The poor man kneeled down and prayed with zeal; and when he was touching on the political state of the country, and praying that Heaven would spare a remnant, Claverhouse, interrupting him, said, *'I gave you leave to pray, and you are preaching.'* — *'Sir,'* answered the prisoner, turning towards his judge on his knees, *'you know nothing either of preaching or praying, if you call what I now say preaching:'* — then continued without confusion. When his devotions were ended, Claverhouse commanded him to bid good-night to his wife and children.

Brown turned towards them, and taking his wife by the hand, told her that the hour was come which he had spoken of when he first asked her consent to marry him. The poor woman answered firmly, — *'In this cause I am willing to resign you.'* "Then have I nothing *to do save to die,'* he replied; *'and I thank God I have been in a frame to meet death for many years.'* He was shot dead by a party of soldiers at the end of his own house; and although his wife was of a nervous habit, and used to become sick at the sight of blood, she had on this occasion strength enough to support the dreadful scene without fainting or confusion, only her eyes dazzled when the carbines were fired. While her husband's dead body lay stretched before him, Claverhouse asked her what she thought of her husband now. *'I ever thought much of him,'* she replied, *'and now more than ever.' 'It were but justice,'* said Claverhouse, *'to lay thee beside him.' 'I doubt not,'* she replied, *'that if you were permitted, your cruelty would carry you that length. But how will you answer for this morning's work?' 'To man I can be answerable,'* said Claverhouse, *'and Heaven I will take in my own hand.'* He then mounted his horse and marched, and left her with the corpse of her husband lying beside her, and her fatherless infant in her arms. *'She placed the child on the ground,'* says the narrative, with scriptural simplicity, 'tied up the corpse's head, and straighted the limbs, and covered him with her plaid, and sat down and wept over him.'"

There are direct descendants of this John Brown still leaving near to the manse in the Kirkton of Blantyre.

The old folk in Blantyre still speak of the Rebellion in 1745 as being "*the Hielandman's year*," for it would seem that "Bonnie Prince Charlie" marched part of his army through the parish, on their way to Carlisle, and the Prince had given orders that none of his soldiers should molest any person or property in Blantyre, as the parish belonged to a "Stuart," alluding to Lord Blantyre. A boy stood at his father's door looking at the wild array as they filed past, and overcoming his fear, he laughed, at their uncouth appearance. That was nearly his last laugh, for a young irascible Highlander plucked out his dagger and flung it, like a javelin, at the boy's head. Luckily it missed him, but struck through a cupboard that stood behind him; and there, to this day, is to be seen the hole it made in the smoke-blackened oak-wood.

There is another relic of that year in the possession of one of our lairds; this is a large square-shaped black bottle with the date upon it 1743. When the "Hielandmen" returned from England they again passed through Blantyre; but alas! their glory had disappeared, they were in straggling batches, foot-sore and famishing, and ready to plunder anything and everywhere. Now, the laird of Bardykes wished to save his property, so he stood at his door with the big black bottle filled with whisky, and a basket of oatmeal cakes, and he gave a glass and a farle to each of the "Hielandmen," who thus pleasantly refreshed, passed on to "lift" some other where.

Mr Moore of Greenhall has a quaint old gold watch, connected with which is the following curious story :— On his march into the south country, Prince Charles Edward, with some of his followers, deviated from his course to visit General Stuart at Torrance Castle, which is situated in East Kilbride, on the borders of Blantyre Parish. The Prince was desirous that his namesake should join him in his enterprise; but General Stuart declined to do so, and declared his loyalty to the reigning House of Hanover. And further, he said that being an officer in the King's army, he could not personally entertain the Prince as a guest in his house. At the same time he would not turn the representative of the Royal House of Stuart from his door; so he requested the Prince, with his retinue, to abide at his castle for the night, and having given orders for their entertainment, he himself sought lodgings elsewhere. In the morning Prince Charles left to join his Highlanders who were bivouacked in the neighbourhood of Hamilton. The general returned to the castle, and found that his watch, which he had inadvertently left on the dressing-table in his bed-room, was gone. Search was made for it, but to no purpose; so the general was reluctantly forced to conclude that some one in the service of the Prince had stolen the watch. He accordingly sent a messenger to Hamilton, with a letter to Prince Charles telling him of the loss. Of course the chivalrous young Prince was greatly annoyed that any of his followers should have so abused the kindly hospitality they had received, by perpetrating such a mean act. He at once called together all who had been with him at Torrance, and promised the man who had committed the theft, a free pardon if he would deliver up the watch. The thief stepped forward, and handed it to the Prince. So the watch was sent back to General Stuart with many expressions of regret.

Mr Moore has likewise in his possession the snuff-box which the gallant general put at the disposal of Prince Charles, and the tablecloth used that night at dinner; it has got sewn upon it the initials of the unfortunate Prince.

Professor Millar of Milheugh and Dr Baillie, minister of Bothwell, afterwards Professor of Divinity, were great friends, and their families lived in the closest intimacy. One of the daughters of the former was very fond of carpentry, and had built for herself a small picturesque bower in the garden beside the river, where "she plied her chosen trade." Joanna Baillie, poetess and dramatist, wrote the following lines upon her friend and her occupation, which are still to be read on the wall of the little house :—

> This is no haunt of contemplation,
> Nor bower in which their dear potation
> Of Eastern herbs fair ladies sip,
> With sparkling eye and glowing lip
> This is the Bower of Industry.
> Yet think not here within to spy
> The silken bag or huswife neat
> On table laid or wicker'd seat.
> No! here the hammer's active din
> Blends with the sound of roaring lin,
> As brawling Calder hastens through
> The shady holms of sweet Milheugh.
> Here from planed board the shavings rise,
> And like sunn'd mists the sawdust flies.
> But scarce a lady of the land
> May own a smaller, fairer hand,
> Than she, who 'neath this roof's cool shade
> Plies fitfully her chosen trade.
> With skilful sleight and eager eye,
> A female Amateur of Carpentry.

JOANNA BAILLIE.

The old road along which Queen Mary passed on her way from Hamilton Palace to Cathcart Castle on the day previous to the battle of Langside, intersects the grounds of Milheugh, near to the house, and there is a beautiful spring of water in an adjoining glen, still known by the name of Queen Mary's Well, at which that unfortunate lady is said to have rested.

Although Calderwood Castle is not in our parish, yet the Baronet, Sir William Maxwell, whose seat it is, is one of our heritors; so the following story may be legitimately included in our parish papers. We are reminded of it by the name of Joanna Baillie :—

The old Castle of Calderwood, which was built on a precipice overlooking the Calder, fell on the morning of the 23rd January, 1773. Its fall and the providential safety of all its inmates are thus narrated in the March number of *Chambers's Journal,* in the year 1833 :— "The fall of this castle, which took place about sixty years ago, was attended with circumstances of so romantic a nature, that we think them deserving of record. There was a Dr Baillie, a clergyman, father of the late Sir Matthew Baillie, physician in London, and who had been tutor to the then Sir William Maxwell and his two brothers, who had a villa in that neighbourhood, and was consequently a frequent visitor at the castle. One day when at dinner with his wife, he said that he had all forenoon felt an anxiety about Calderwood, as if some of the family were ill. Mrs Baillie said there seemed no cause for such a supposition, and the conversation ended. At tea in the evening Dr Baillie said, "You know, Mrs Baillie, that I am not superstitious, but it is strongly impressed on my mind that some of that family is seriously ill." Mrs Baillie replied that had this been the case he might be sure that they would have been informed of the circumstance; besides, he was down there five days before, when they were all in perfect health. At the supper Dr Baillie again said, "It does not signify, Mrs Baillie, but I have taken an anxiety about that family that I can neither account for nor control, and I am certain that some individual there is seriously ill."

Mrs Baillie desired him to order his horse to the door, and put his night-cap into his pocket, and ride down to the castle, though the family would be much surprised at a visit at so late an hour. Dr Baillie arrived about eleven o'clock, when the family were just going to bed. His first question was, "Is the family all well?" Lady Maxwell said they were all well, thank God, and was glad to see the doctor, and ordered a bed-room to be prepared for him. He then explained the cause of so untimely a visit, and requested Sir William that he would order a servant with a couple of candles to go with him into the castle while his bed-room was preparing, as he wished to examine the east wall, where he perceived a slight rent when he was last there, and was desirous to see if any alteration had since taken place. It may be proper to say that all the house-servants and several of the farm-servants slept in the castle, and most of them had gone to bed. In about a quarter of an hour Dr Baillie returned, and said he was certain the castle was going to fall, as the rent he had formerly noticed was considerably enlarged. The servants were all ordered to get out of bed and join the family, who resided in a more modern building attached to the castle.

At the top of the castle was a square tower in which were deposited the archives and records of the family. These Sir William had conveyed away. The family then determined to sit up all night and see the result; when at half-past nine in the morning the whole of the east side of the castle went over with a tremendous crash. There was a range of stables below the castle, where there were some horses, but these were saved, by the stables being arched, and were dug out of the ruins two days afterwards. Thus if it had not been for a providential interposition of Dr Baillie nine or ten persons would have been crushed to death."

In the middle of last century, a lad named William Pollock emigrated from High Blantyre to America. He was one of the sons of Archibald Pollock, blacksmith in Kirkton, where he was born, according to the old Parish Register, in the 27th December, 1735. Arrived in Virginia, William followed his father's trade for many years, and prospered so well that in 1782, on the 15th of April, he wrote to his father (the old letter is now before us), telling of his success in life, how he had amassed a considerable fortune, and bought an estate, and married a wife, and had seven children. And the postscript is as follows :—

"*The following is a small sketch of my estate — 14 negroes, 12,000 acres of land, beside a large stock of flour and meat cattle.*" And here is another quotation from another of those old letters — it was written by John, the son of the above-mentioned William, and is dated Fredericksburg, 18th March, 1790 :— "*My father has the old number of children — eight, and the youngest is a son, which he has called after his brother James, and is prouder of him than of all the others. There is a numerous family of Blacks, which is very expensive. The grain crop is larger than ever was put into the ground in one year. All other provisions are lower and plentier than ever they have been."*

Now this American family of Pollock, from some whim or other, changed their name to Polk; and a grandson of the young blacksmith who emigrated from Blantyre was James Knox Polk, one of the ablest and most distinguished of the Presidents of the United States of America. He was elected in 1844, and during his administration many important events happened, bearing on the fortunes of the Republic. "By the annexation of Texas and California he extended the boundaries of the States, and introduced into Government many financial and commercial improvements. He died in 1849." Another descendant, and cousin of the President, was Leonidas Polk, a Bishop of the Episcopal Church. On the breaking out of the Civil War he laid aside his bishop's mitre, and joined the Confederate Army. He rose to the rank of General, having greatly distinguished himself.

Unfortunately, he was killed by a shot, as the war was just terminating, in June, 1864.

The longevity of the old inhabitants of Blantyre was wonderful, and the simplicity of their lives was great. As a rule, they were content with their little, and were not ambitious to wander away to distant parts. William Greig, dead lately, had never been out of the parish for eighty years, and never for one night out of his own bed for fifty years, and he was only one of the many who could say the same thing. We remember an old woman of the same age assuring us that she had never been out of Blantyre all her lifetime, except one day when a girl she walked into Glasgow in the morning, and back again at night; and another octogenarian is said to have strayed once so far from the village as the heights of Auchintibber, when, after looking intently upon the rich and wide valley before her, she was heard to say, "Weel, I never thocht that the world was so large afore." This, however, we are inclined to think, may be apocryphal. The following, however, is quite true :— An old laird, who is still living, was never, but once, within another church save the Parish Church of Blantyre, and of it he was a regular attendant during a long life, until age and infirmity came upon him.

On a recent visit to London we saw the celebrated painting by Mrs Butler (Miss Thomson), entitled, "Scotland for ever!" It represents the famous charge of the Scots Greys at Waterloo, which drew from the lips of Napoleon the exclamation, "Ces terribles Chevaux gris; comme travaillent!" The picture reminded us of a letter we wrote to the *Glasgow Herald* two years ago, and which we here transcribe :—

"Sir, in those days when the martial spirit is so prominent amongst the young men of our country, it will not be deemed unwelcome if you should present to them an interesting memorial of 'the brave days of old.' In my parish there is an old man, now bed-ridden through age, who had two brothers that were present at the battle of Waterloo — the one was a sergeant and the other a corporal in the Scots Greys. On retiring from the army, the former abode in England, but the latter came back to his native village, where he lived for a few years longer and died. This corporal, Robert Thomson, was so tall and heavy, that a special horse had to be got for him. In the famous charge of the regiment this horse was killed by the bursting of a shell, which likewise wounded the rider, who fell to the ground, his dead horse above him. After the battle he was found and rescued, with other three comrades, who had been tossed over by the same deadly missile, two of them being 92nd Highlanders. For it will be remembered that the Highland foot soldiers, vehemently excited, breaking their ranks, and catching hold of the stirrups of the Scots Greys, joined in the charge, shouting, 'Scotland for ever!' The corporal left to his brother the Waterloo medal, which is still a cherished heirloom, and along with it is an old yellow time-stained paper, containing a printed copy of the colonel's address to his regiment on presenting the medals to the men. This address is one of the finest of its kind, and deserves to be rescued from oblivion :—

Address to the Second or Royal North British Regiment of Dragoons, by Lieut.-Colonel Clark.

"I have the pleasure this day of delivering to the regiment these medals, as a mark of the approbation of your Prince, and the applause of your country, for your gallant conduct on that memorable day which they are intended to perpetuate — a duty to me the most gratifying which has fallen to my lot since I have had the honour of commanding one of the finest, I had almost been tempted to say the finest, regiment of cavalry in the British service, whose well-known valour needs no comment from an humble individual like me — its fame is registered in the hearts of all men, and its name will live revered and respected as long as history remains. May happiness be yours, and may you live long to enjoy these honourable badges; may they stimulate those who wear them to further acts of bravery whenever their services shall be called for; and may their bright example stimulate the recruit.

At this moment I feel but one regret, that it is not in my power to present every man in the regiment with a medal; but let not those who are excluded from the honour feel the slightest uneasiness (I now allude to those serving at the depot). We all know that their hearts panted to share the glories of the day, but the various duties on which they were employed at home were of the highest magnitude; and we must also recollect that many of them were actually engaged in providing comforts for their comrades on service. It remains only for me to make one request — that every man will religiously treasure his medal, given to him by the Prince Regent, in the name and on the behalf of His Majesty, as a testimony of his most gracious approbation of their well-earned fame; let them guard their precious gift to the latest hour of their lives, and when summoned from this to a better world, let them bequeath it to their children, who will proudly exclaim, "This was my Father's, who gained immortal honour at the Battle of Waterloo" — "This was my Father's, who gloriously assisted in giving peace to Europe" — "This was my Father's, who helped to hurl the tyrant Bonaparte from the Throne of France to the Rock of St. Helena."

About a hundred years ago, or thereabouts, the laird of Shott was returning from Hamilton at the close of a market day. Whether it was from the fatigues of the day, or owing to the cold of the night, the laird fell asleep, and unfortunately fell out of his one-horse shay; but falling "saftly," as the folks said, he lay still where he was, to have his forty winks. And the faithful beast, accustomed to such pranks of his master, stood quietly by till the laird should awaken. Two strangers came along the road, and seeing what appeared a terrible catastrophe, they anxiously bent over the prostrate man, to find if there was life in him; and finding that he breathed, they tried to rouse him, telling him to get up, and asking him, "Who are you? Who are you?" At last they got a reply, "I'm Shott, I'm Shott." "Who shot you?" "I'm Shott at Blantyre." The men were good Samaritans, and so they gently lifted the *wounded* man into his own gig, and drove him back to Hamilton, where they roused up the police at the station-house, told of the tragedy, and delivered over their charge. But to the consternation of the strangers, no sooner did the lantern flash its light upon the "wounded" man's face, than the police burst into loud laughter, telling the benevolent Samaritans, "It's only old Shott, the laird, at Blantyre." We are of opinion that those kindly individuals would make a pretty minute examination the next time they saw a man prostrate by the wayside.

One would scarcely expect to find amongst the worthy Blantyre Lairds a Disciple of Pythagoras, one who firmly believed in the transmigration of souls. Such there was, however, about half a century ago. He had many eccentricities, and this was one which he cherished to the last, for on his deathbed he said to his family, "You needna expec' that I'll be lang awa frae Woodlea, I loo it too weel for that. So when simmer comes, and ye hear the blackbird singing in the branches oot there, mind ye, *that's me.*"

It was before the days of the Hamilton provincial newspaper, with its many advertising columns, when the Beadle of Blantyre was wont to make known any current events by "crying" them at the Church door on Sunday, as the people were "skailing." A sure method certainly to dissipate any good impressions produced by the worthy minister's sermon, for some of these proclamations were very queer. At one time it would be a hay stack, or a field of beans to be sold; or the hind quarter of a "Mairt" to be disposed of; or that Lord Blantyre's factor was to be up on such a day to gather the rents. Here is one of them verbatim, *"This is to give notice that there was found on the Sides an empty sack with a cheese at the bottom of it, whoever has lost the same, by applying to me will get it."*

We have already alluded to the longevity of the natives; here is an instance of it. There have been only three beadles of the parish for one hundred and twenty years, each of them holding the office for almost the exact same period of forty years. Peggy Haddo was the daughter of the beadle of the last century who was wont to make the public intimations at the Kirk door. She died a short time ago at the advanced age of ninety-two. For several years before her death she never lighted a candle in her cottage, and when asked by her kindly landlord how she spent the long winter evenings, not able to read, she replied, "You see, sir, when I was a lassie herding the cows in the fields below, I learned by heart the first forty-five psalms and the CXIX Psalm, and now every night in my old age I go over these again and again, and that's my delight." When she was dying, a young minister visited her and asked if he would read a portion of scripture. "O aye," she said, and specified the fourteenth chapter of St. John. The minister read, and thinking that she had fallen asleep he made a pause, but the old woman, rocking herself to and fro, said feebly but earnestly, "Don't stop, don't stop, its gran', its gran'." A few hours more, and Peggy passed away to realise, far above what eye had seen or ear heard, or tongue been able to tell, how grand was the Saviour's assurance, "In my father's house are many resting-places, I go to prepare a place for you."

Old Robin was once the "Minister's man," and of course had charge of the "Manse Garden." But although he watched carefully against all depredators, he was a tender-hearted man, and thought it no great sin if, once, in a way during the season, the boys of the village should taste of the Minister's apples and gooseberries. Accordingly on the privileged night he would assemble them round his door, and they waited there until the *gun* went off. This was the Minister, having finished his studies he went out at the front door, and standing in the garden walk he fired off an old blunderbuss to frighten away all thieves. "Now," said Robin to the boys, "let us go in, the Minister is gone to bed." And so in they went, and came safely out, with their pockets stuffed full with fruit from the well stocked orchard.

The small property of Auchinraith, originally called Whistleberry, on which the house is built, was once in the possession of Captain Lockhart, who was for long the popular M.P. for Lanarkshire. By him it was sold in 1831, when he inherited the beautiful property of Milton Lockhart. Sir Walter Scott was a frequent guest of his friend and relation at both of these places, and it was during those visits that he picked up much of his material for his romance "Old Mortality," the locality of which is almost entirely at "Tillietudlem" and "Bothwell Brig." Our readers who are acquainted with the topography of Craighead and its environs will easily recognise those in the graphic and matchless description which Sir Walter gives of the place he calls "Fairy Knowe." It is a beautiful picture of part of our parish.

"It was on a delightful summer evening, that a stranger, well mounted, and having the appearance of a military man of rank, rode down a winding descent which terminated in view of the romantic ruins of Bothwell Castle and the river Clyde, which winds so beautifully between rocks and woods to sweep around the towers formerly built by Aymer de Valence. Bothwell Bridge was at a little distance and also in sight. The opposite field, once the scene of slaughter and conflict, now lay as placid and quiet as the surface of a summer lake. The trees and bushes, which grew around in romantic variety of shade, were hardly seen to stir under the influence of the evening breeze. The very murmur of the river seemed to soften itself into unison with the stillness of the scene around.

"The path, through which the traveller descended, was occasionally shaded by detached trees of great size, and elsewhere by the hedges and boughs of flourishing orchards, now laden with summer fruits. The nearest object of consequence was a farmhouse, or, it might be, the abode of a small proprietor, situated on the side of a sunny bank, which was covered by apple and pear trees. At the foot of the path which led up to this modest mansion was a small cottage, pretty much in the situation of a porter's lodge, though obviously not designed for such a purpose. The hut seemed comfortable, and more neatly arranged than is usual in Scotland. It had its little garden, where some fruit trees and bushes were mingled with kitchen herbs; a cow and six sheep fed in a paddock hard by; the cock strutted and crowed, and summoned his family around him before the door; a heap of brushwood and turf, neatly made up, indicated that the winter fuel was provided, and the thin blue smoke which ascended from the straw bound chimney, and winded slowly out from among the green trees, showed that the evening meal was in the act of being made ready. To complete the rural scene of peace and comfort, a girl of about five years of age was fetching water in a pitcher from a beautiful fountain of the purest transparency, which bubbled up at the root of a decayed old oak tree, about twenty yards from the end of the cottage.

"The stranger reined up his horse, and called to the little nymph, desiring to know the way to Fairy-Knowe. The child set down her water pitcher, hardly understanding what was said to her, put her fair flaxen hair apart on her brows, and opened her round blue eyes with the wondering, 'What's your wull?' which is usually a peasant's first answer, if it can be called one, to all questions whatever. "'I wish to know the way to Fairy-Knowe.'"

Since this book has gone to press, we have received the following most interesting information regarding a Prior of Blantyre, from a valued correspondent, Joseph Bain, Esq., of Fulham, London, who has edited for the Treasury the Calendar of Documents relating to Scotland now in the Public Record Office.

"Edward I., by writ dated Wemyss, in Fife, 5th March, 1303-4, commands the Sheriff of Lanark to cause Robert de Barde (Baird), who was distraining the pledges for the ransom of Friar William de Cokeburyne, Warden of Blantyre Priory, to desist as this was in violation of the conditions on which John Comyn the Regent and his adherents had surrendered to the King. It is evident this Friar had been an adherent of Comyn, and Baird had made him prisoner on the King's behalf, and was holding him to ransom. Strange to say, the then Sheriff of Lanark was Robert Bruce!"

Mr. Bain likewise makes the following remarks as to the successor of the Earl of March and "Black Agnes," which accords not with accepted history. "It is almost proved that George, the 'great rebel,' was not the son of Earl Patrick and 'Black Agnes,' but of another Patrick and a sister of hers. In fact if he had been Earl Patrick's *son*, the resignation of the Earldom to him would have been meaningless. This striking mistake has been caused by the abbreviation of the Great Seal Register. There is also good evidence tending to show that David Dunbar, first of Cumnock and Blantyre (by Earl George's grant of 1374) was the descendant of John Dunbar, a brother of the Earl, who died in 1308, and whose direct representatives are the present Sir William Dunbar of Mochrum, and Mr Dunbar of Northfield."

By Rev Stewart Wright

LIST OF THE HERITORS OF THE PARISH OF BLANTYRE

Arranged according to the value of their land

The Right Honourable Lord Blantyre

Mrs George Scott, of Blantyre Farm

John Clark Forrest, of Auchinraith

John Craig, of Bellsfield

Sir W. A. Maxwell (trustees), of Calderwood

John Macpherson, of Blantyre Farm

John Jackson, of Bardykes

John Jackson (trustees), of Barnhill

James Naismith, of Coatshill

William Gardiner, of Priestfield

J. Wardrop Moore, of Greenhall

Robert Murdoch, of West Haughhead

William Carrick Anderson, Calderside

George Alston (trustees), Craighead

Joseph Francis Monteath, Carstairs

Mrs Bannatyne, of Milheugh

The Right Honourable the Earl of Home, Blantyre Priory

John Gardiner, of Newmains

Colonel Harrington Stuart, Torrance

William Mather, of Shott

Archd. Craig (trustees), of Birdsfield

Mrs Christina Murdoch, of East Haughhead

John Coats, of Blantyre Farm

Thomas Scott, of Priestfield

Thomas Ripley Ker, of Auchinraith

Thos. Jackson, of Blantyre Park

Mrs Janet Jackson, of Springwell

Wm. Jackson, of Blantyre Park

John Torrance Weir, of Blantyre Park

John Richard Cochrane, of Calder Glen

John Dickson, of Newfield

John Dennistoun, of Hartfield

William Jackson and trustees of Thos. Jackson, Croftfoot

James Hamilton, of Newhouse

John Russell, of Muirfoot

Colin Dunlop & Co

Mrs Betsy Weir, of Gooseholm

Rev. Stewart Wright, the Glebe

James Clelland Burns, of Glenlee

Robert Craig (heirs of), of Barnhill

Mrs Strang Watkins, of Calder-bank

Arthur Leggate, of Springpark

Mrs Eliz. Coats, of Stonefield

Caledonian Railway Company

APPENDIX.

In compiling this book I have had many old and interesting papers kindly placed at my disposal by Mrs Scott of Blantyre-ferme. They refer to Parish matters, Civil and Ecclesiastical, from the commencement of the seventeenth century, and were the property of the "Baron-Baillies," which office, as I have already stated, was held successively by the Hamiltons of Ferme-Blantyre. For the deciphering of some of these papers, not an easy task, I am indebted to Mr Bain.

As a specimen of them, let me mention three that are now before me. Here is a judgment passed in the Barony Court of Blantyre held at the Mansion House in the month of May, 1606, by the Right Hon. James Dunlop of that ilk, Baillie, and is in the handwriting of a "George Hucheson, Notar," who, Mr Bain alleges, was the same gentleman that was the founder of the Hospital in Glasgow which bears his name. The judgment seems to have been the result of a petition put forward by Lord Blantyre, on his coming into possession of the Barony, to see and examine the title-deeds of the vassals who had acquired their lands from the Dunbars of Enterkin and Blantyre. Walter Lord Blantyre appeared personally at this court, and the Feuars through their "Preloquitor, Thomas Wilson." Parties being heard and the Judge "weile and ryplie advisit," "the said Bailyie decerns and ordains that the writs, etc., not producit, are null and void, and of no effect in or outwith judgment in all tyme coming," etc. Two intervening Courts, on 17th May and "Feird" March, had been held, the latter of the feuars' own naming, and as they had failed to appear and produce their writs, the judge decerns against them (*not signed*).

The second paper is a most interesting document, being an agreement between the Rev. John Heriot "prior joynt minister" of Blantyre, and Mr James Hamilton, appointed his "colleg" by the Presbytery of Hamilton to "serve along with Mr John in the officc of minister and service of the cuire in the Paroch Kirk." The document is dated at Blantyre Kirk on 6th February, 1654, and in it the "prior minister" agrees to provide his "colleg" in the equal half of the stipend of "40 bolls meill, 16 bolls beir, and 450 merks of money," payable as follows :—

MEILL	Bolls	Pecks	Leipies	
" "	1	6	1½	"dew" by Wm. Hamilton of Blantyre ferme
" "	0	9½	½	James Arbuckle in Greinhall
" "	4	0	0	John Lindsay, elder in Blantyre ferm
" "	4	0	0	John Somer, in foote of the toun of Blantyre ferm
" "	4	0	0	John Arbuckle and Janet Miller, in Blantyre ferm, Equally betwix thaim
" "	6	0	0	James Trumble in Blantyre ferm

BEIR	Furlottes	Pecks	
" "	6	6¼	The tenants and posssessours of lands of Auchinraith
" "	0	6	James Lindsay of Bardisdykes
" "	3	0	John Jacksone of Bardisdykes
" "	1	0	James Smith at the Kirk of Blantyre

BEIR	Bolls	Pecks	Leipies	
" "	1	0	0	"dew" be John Lindsay, elder in Blantyre ferm.
" "	2	0	0	James Trumble, there.
" "	1	0	0	Wm. Somer, at toun foote there.
" "	0	15½	½	James Thomson in . . . . .

MONEY.   225 merks dew be Lord of Blantyre All for Crop and Year 1653.

Mr Hamilton accepts these in full of all demands for his "service and functione of the ministrie" in the parish during Mr John's lifetime. Mr John obliges himself to pay his "colleg" 20 merks to help him to buy communion elements when the communion is to be administered — if not administered, then Mr John to be freed. Mr James obliges himself and his successors in the parish to pay to the relict or assigneys of Mr John, "gif it sall pleis God to call upon ye said Mr John in the said Mr James his tyme of function and servand the cuire," 600 merks Scottis in full satisfaction of the manse and gleib.

This curious document was witnessed "by James and Thomas Herriott, sons lawful to Mr John," William Pollock at Blantyre Kirk, and John Rowat there; and was registered in the Court books of Edinburgh on 13th February, 1656.

The third document is a most remarkable one, the existence of which will take everyone connected with the district by surprise. It is an Extract Decreet by the Lords Commissioners of Surrenders and Teinds, of date 1634, disjoining the "toun" and lands of Crossbasket from East Kilbride, and incorporating them with the Parish of Blantyre. This Decreet has never been carried into effect, but why, it is impossible now to say. Yet here it is *verbatim* :—

Extract Decreet by the Lords Commissioners of Surrenders and Teinds, on the Summons raised by Patrick Archbishop of Glasgow, the Diocesan, Sir Thomas Hope of Craighall, Knt. barronett H.M.'s Advocate, and Mr John Heriot, Minister of Blantyre, against Wm. lord Blantyre, Titular of the teinds, John Hamiltoun of Westoun, Robert Hamiltoun of Torence, Wm. Hamiltoun of Blanterferme, John Hamiltoun of Casslane, Bothwell, Robert Hamiltoun of Newhouse, James Baillie of Park, Robert Hammiltoun at the Kirk of Blantyre, Janet Miller and James Arbuckell her son, in Pithheid of Corsbasket, Wm. Jackstoun in Barnhill, John Miller, thair, John Watson, thair, Claud Hammiltoun, thair, John Clerke in Achinreithe, John Strutheris in Achinreithe, Tutor to Johne Watson in Barnhill, John Clerk in Achinreth, John Clerk, thair, John Clerk, thair, James Clerk in Stanslide, tutor to John Clerk, Wm. Hammiltoun of Schott, John and James Craigie in Auchenraithe, David Corss in Flemyngtoun and John Thomson in Sydis, heritors of the lands in Blantyre. [Necessity of an augmentation declared, etc.]

"And becaus the toun and landis of Crossbasket, place and maynor yairof, and greine lyand within the parochine of Kilbryde are contigue and mare adjacent to the said paroche Kirk and parochine of Blantyre, within one quarter of ane mylle or theireby, the inhabitants of the quhilk toun and landis being neare two mylles distant from their awin paroche Kirk, doe always resort and repair to the said Kirk of Blantyre, quhair they ar onlie servit, so that the said Mr John Heriot has the only chairge of these inhabitants, and thairfore for the weill and ease of these people it evidentlie appeirit to be necessar that the saidis roumes and landis sud be dissolvit and disuneite from the said parochine of Kilbryde and annexit and uneit to the parochine of Blantyre." [Clauses as to noncompearment

125

defenders held as confesture.]

Action called and parties appearing, the minister, "be John Pitcarne and Mr David Heriot, advocattes and proloquitors, quha divysit that as no *money rent* is payit within the parochine," the Commissioners would count the augmentation of 8 bolls beir and 24 bolls meile (2 chalders) into 100 pundis money, besides £10 for communion elements, Lord Blantyre by his prior Mr James Aikenheid, advocate, consented to same, and the Lords Commissioners decreed accordingly.

Edinburgh, 15th December, 1634.

By Rev Stewart Wright

ABOUT THE TRANSCRIBER

Paul D Veverka is a Blantyre born businessman, Commercial Construction manager, local historian and author. He has an active and growing interest in all aspects of History and improving community life in his hometown of Blantyre. As a day job, his construction managerial activities have in recent years included the construction of the new Queensferry Crossing over the Forth and the large 58km Aberdeen bypass Road.

Born in 1971, Paul is the eldest of four children of Josef and Janet Veverka (both dec.) from whom he inherited his passion for the history of Blantyre. With Scottish maternal ancestry and Czech paternal ancestry, he is Chairperson of Blantyre Community Committee and a self confessed community campaigner for all sorts of improvements in his home town. His successful non profit website *"The Blantyre Project"* is currently attracting widespread regard from ex-pats & local residents alike and followed daily by over 12,000 people. Paul resides at Croftfoot, High Blantyre, itself one of Blantyre's oldest inhabited houses dating from 1730. His wife, Paula is a Professional Wedding Photographer based at the studio adjacent and they have a much adored, five year old daughter, Annalily.

Paul's passion for Blantyre history has seen him post articles online about Blantyre each and every day since 2011 and working away from home often, he has found time to publish five successful books about Blantyre, since then.

"Without the warm stories of Blantyre's history and heritage, without unconditional kindness to neighbours and creating a sense of community pride and understanding that <u>this</u> is where we are from, we would truly have nothing of any real, lasting value to pass to our children."

Paul Veverka, February 2017

Made in the USA
Charleston, SC
09 February 2017